Book One of the Complete Humanity Series

BUDDHA ON A BULL

A Practical Approach to Enlightenment

ELENA NEZHINSKY

Forewords by Chris Grosso & Nurit and Gabor Harsanyi

Published by Awaken Now Publishing

Book cover/logo design by Bonnie Aungle

Illustrations by Jason Kolano

Internal design by Jane Green of Everlasting Magic Design.
www.everlastingmagicdesign.com

ISBN — 978-1-7332220-0-6

To everyone

who is tired of seeking enlightenment,

like I was...

RIDING THE BULL
FIELD NOTES

For confused beings like ourselves who have the habit of shopping from shelf to shelf for Dharma snacks, Elena has written the perfect handbook. If you've been gorging on empty calories, here is the balanced nutritional supplement you need. And it answers many of the modern problems never even thought of in Traditional Eastern meditation texts! It's practical, and gives advice on avoiding difficulties, which are all of our own making. And it's simple, full of easy effective ways to make sure that once we get unstuck, we can relax, free.

--John Hoag, Practitioner of Dzogchen and translator for Tibetan Teachers, Montana, USA and Nepal

She invites us to wake up right where we are. To allow the knowingness to show up: there is no need to try to find it. It is organic, not a static view, just follow your heart, be still, and in the silence the struggle will settle to a realization of one's true nature. Just be. I felt the panic of my heart calm reading her words. Her poetics and insight from a long journey paid off. I love her and her story.

--Jane Edberg, MFA, former Professor of Art at Gavilan College, California, USA

'OH MY F-ING GOD!! This is the most real, raw, wild, truthful, funny book on awakening and enlightenment I have ever read. It could easily be called 'welcome to being human'. Elena brings the spiritual search into the realm of being human in a way that no one else could. I deeply and highly recommend this easy to read, easy to love, easy to understand jewel to anyone seeking themselves.

--Shanti Zimmermann, Emotional Clarity Mentor, Switzerland

The writing is simplicity itself, in her unique enjoyable voice she speaks to her readers as an equal, without the rarified air of a teacher, daring them to let go of everything they think they know about seeking, about enlightenment, and about who they really are. Accessible and beautifully devoid of non-dual BS.

--Cynthia M. Clingan, MSEd, PCC, Somatic Psychotherapist, Ohio, USA

Elena has written a delightful guide full of important pointers for those who wish to explore the journey of awakening. The book is easy to read and the stories are told with sincere honesty, eliminating the many fantasies surrounding spirituality. Her practical guide will lead the readers to discover that the ordinary life when free from compartmentalization is exactly where and when the search ends and what comes after is a human life that is free and full of wonder and amazement.

--John Tan "Thusness", Dharma Teacher featured in the Awakening to Reality blog project, Singapore

A joy to read. It's like sitting in a coffee shop with a friend who has awakened, chatting in an easy, relaxed, fun way while listening to stories and anecdotes, jokes and wisdom of the way home, back to your true self, and discovering you have always been there.

--Vinito Freo, Non-Dual Therapist, Australia

A fascinating tale of seeking and finding, laden with insight, helpful perspectives and refreshing candor. Many will find inspiration and practical pointers to assist their own spiritual search through Elena's eloquent charting of the peaks and troughs of her heroine's journey. Here is a genuinely fresh and authentic voice in a crowded marketplace.

--Will Pye, author of *The Gratitude Prescription*, founder of Love & Truth Party, Australia

Elena has written a passionate story of her love affair with Truth, that is an exquisite invitation for all those with this interest. Thoroughly enjoyed and appreciated!

--Isaac Shapiro, non-duality teacher, Australia

Buddha on a Bull is forthright, raw, playful, vulnerable, and daring. To feel accompanied on the path to self-understanding, to know the value of your quest for transformation, lean into the words and wisdom of Elena Nezhinsky. She gleans from her years of searching. A book unlike any other.

--Patrice Vecchione, author of *Step into Nature: Nurturing Imagination and Spirit in Everyday Life*, California, USA

Elena unapologetically follows an inner knowing. Listening and following one's inner knowing, she informs the reader, is imperative as the ultimate guide home. In her book, *Buddha On a Bull*, Elena displays the courage, insight, and understanding gained from her life journey, and she generously shares her experiencesand guideposts with the reader.

--Susanne Marie, Spiritual Mentor and Guide, New Mexico, USA

This is raw, honest, personal testimony. I particularly enjoyed the light-hearted directness and the down-to-earth, practical approach of the second part of the book, so much of which resonates with my own journey and experience. The ending slows down magically, echoing the slowing down and disappearance of 'I'. Beautifully expressed!

--Mark Marshall with Frederic Constant, founders of nondualityforum.com, France

Loved being taken by Elena on 'her train'. Beautifully written. Honest, clear and raw... Wonderful!

--Meike Schutt, non-duality teacher, Australia

To read Elena's words is to travel alongside the ultimate spiritual friend, to listen deeply and watch understanding and recognition arise in you. Elena writes with clarity, courage, humor, and compassion about her own experience of waking up. *Buddha on a Bull* stirs the truth within, the place in each of us that already knows. It is a book that can change you!

--Jane Murphy, Editor, Writing Coach, Oregon, USA

I recognize something in here that is rare to see, and that is realness, pure honest witness filled with grace and tenacity.
--Sjef Romijn, Human Design teacher, writer at "Reflector Sessions", Netherlands

A must-read book for all spiritual seekers! Her writing is refreshingly direct and honest!
--Cynthia Copple, Ayurvedic Doctor, author of *Know your Blueprint*, California, USA

An easy read for someone interested in truth but in no way is it a simple book, you will find abundant nuggets of wisdom and many warnings about possible pitfalls along the way.
--Magdi Badawi, Non-duality teacher, Virginia, USA

In sharing the intimate details of her awakening journey, with a beautiful energetic lightness and laughter at the absurdity of it all, Elena provides a set of bread crumbs to follow. I saw my personal journey in many of her stories and found myself constantly smiling at what was shared.
--Fergus Denhamer VP Operations, Vancouver, Canada

Buddha on a Bull is a wonderful, heartfelt journey on a train that takes you to the station you never really left, your own Awakened Consciousness. Elena's genuineness, sincerity, and humility shine and invite you along for the ride.
--Ishtar Howell, Meditation teacher, Ishaya monk, Oregon, USA and Portugal

Buddha on a Bull is able to capture the exhilarating and difficult ride of spiritual transformation and awakening. It's an encouraging and enlightening read on the winding spiritual path.
--Joan Staffen, author of *The Book of Pendulum Healing*, California USA

Buddha on a Bull book has a great purpose. I have known Elena's work for many years and recommend her message for all to read and learn from.
--Shane Wilson, Buddhist teacher, The Meditation Learning Center, Arizona USA

Waking up is such an individual expedition! *Buddha on a Bull* provide practical, yet profound insights for spiritual seekers! Reading such experiential and embodied wisdom was a joy!
--Lisa Meuser, MSW, Somatic Therapist, Matrix-Trauma Integration, Indiana, USA

Whether you are new to spiritual inquiry or well established in practice, *Buddha on the Bull* is an unusually candid and penetrating guide, not only to the life-altering experience of waking from the trance of the separate self, but also to the ongoing adventure of embodying the vastness of your true nature in every arena of life.
--Keith Thompson, author of *To Be a Man: In Search of the Deep Masculine*, California, USA

Filled with practical and exhilarating truth, this book just might wake you up!
--Lori Lothian, Astrologer and creator of the Awakened Dreamer blog, Montreal, Canada

TABLE OF CONTENTS

PART 1. THE END OF THE SEARCH. MY STORY AND REFLECTIONS.

Chapter 3. Enlightenment

PART 2. PRACTICAL GUIDANCE TOWARDS ENLIGHTENMENT: MAP AND DIRECTIONS

Chapter 4. Clearing some Doubts, Opening the View

Chapter 5. How to Start, Right Where You Are

Chapter 6. What Tools are Good to Have?

Chapter 7. What to Avoid

Chapter 8. How to Dip into Enlightenment, Now!

ABOUT THE COMPLETE HUMANITY SERIES

Initially I intended to write one book about my own journey of seeking enlightenment and waking up to a true nature of being. I also wanted to include some guidance and tips to help other seekers wake up. While working on this project I discovered that there is a certain passage that can't be hurried or rushed through in order to finish. This passage involves integrating the new perspective, worldview and energies that inevitably come with awakening. It has to be given time, as much time as it will take. So instead of writing one single book to cover the rest of my life I decided to release what I have already written as a part of what will become a trilogy:

Book 1: *Buddha on a Bull: A Practical Aproach to Enlightenement* - this book is about waking up from the illusion of separation and dropping the seeker identity. It covers my own fourteen-year journey from 1998 to 2012 and very practical guide how to wake up.

Book 2: *Dark Night of the Soul: An Alchemy of the Great Unrest* - this book is about the integration of awakening and the releasing of core personality fixations. It covers the seven-year journey from 2012 to 2019 and guidance after awakening.

Book 3: *The Way of Love: Living Unapologetically as I AM* - this book is about the maturation of awakening and what it means to live an awakened life. It covers the journey I am on right now.

There may be other books that will come out in between.

Please enjoy this first book and know that it is part of a series. I am working at this very moment to bring you the next book as soon as possible.

ABOUT THE BOOK COVER

The book's title, *Buddha on a Bull*, came to
me while I was contemplating a way to combine the
spiritual and mundane parts of human existence
into a single image; that is, how to portray embodied
enlightenment. I decided to make a collage. As I
arranged different images somehow the image of
the Buddha (cut out from a *Yoga Journal* magazine,
of cause!) landed on an image of the famous New
York City Wall Street bull sculpture (found in
Forbes magazine)! Boom! The combined image was
powerful and provocative and reflected a part of
my nature: the ability to stir up the mind and move
it beyond its habitual thinking. Working with a
graphic designer friend, we came up with this image
of enlightenment that captures an open luminous
awareness that is our nature and is so ever-present

that it shines equally everywhere, even through Wall Street!

Once, in a Zen monastery, I saw a series of early Chinese calligraphy paintings depicting the seeker's path to enlightenment. The title of this series is sometimes translated into English as "Ten Bulls" with the seeker portrayed as a man and what he seeks—enlightenment—portrayed as a bull.

In these ancient illustrations the man is initially seen looking at some footsteps. As he follows them he sees the bull. Next he catches the bull's tail and tames the animal. He rides the bull home. At the end of the journey the man is in a marketplace, an indication that enlightenment is not separate from living in the world as a human being.

Both images—the Buddha on a Bull and the "Ten Bulls" series—have been a profound source of inspiration for this book. This is a book about searching for, finding, and living awake, not in a Himalayan cave, not removed from the world but in the middle of life's marketplace, *right where you are.*

FOREWORD BY CHRIS GROSSO

Buddha On A Bull is some very real shit.
It's a radically clear, concise, and easily accessible
book about the nature of what many have come to
call "spirituality," the process of "awakening," and
"enlightenment". I intentionally put those words
in quotations because that's all they are, words.
As Elena so eloquently points out in this book, it's
all about direct experience—and not even your
experience—but rather, the experience of life life-
ing itself through the physical vessel which is your
namesake.

This is not to disregard the importance
of honoring our humanity during the process of

awakening to that which is beyond strictly our limited, finite self. I believe this is an important point to make because so much of the non-duality movement has become fixated on things like transcending, or striving to live from a state of constant abiding in non-dual state. There of course is nothing wrong with either the aforementioned, but what happens for many people is they tend to have an unbalanced, mind-based approach to their spiritual practice/life, often negating the human body and all that it encompasses. In some cases, even viewing our bodies as some kind of hindrance that stands in the way of awakening or enlightenment.

Whelp, I've got news for you friends. If it wasn't for these bodies in the first place, this wouldn't even be a topic of debate or discussion. Yes, being human can suck royally and be virtually unbearable, which is why the temptation to take a predominately mind-based spiritual approach, whether consciously or not, is understandable. Hell, who wouldn't want to escape the ugliness of humanity at times, let alone feel all blissed out with no cares in the world.

Elena's approach to awakening, however, honors many aspects of the deeply rooted, traditional approach to non-duality and enlightenment, yet she's carved her own path. Elena isn't afraid to shine a light on outdated paradigms that often instill unrealistic expectations in people regarding their spiritual journey's and what the hell they're actually getting themselves into. The importance of this can't be overstated as it often leaves people feeling jaded and, in some cases, turns them completely off to the whole idea of spirituality, awakening, or whatever you care to call (again, remember, they're just words). Instead, Elena keeps it real, raw, and authentic in every single chapter of this book, promising nothing, yet offering everything.

From discussing the teachings of Gurdjieff to Adyashanti, Jed McKenna (and more), as well as her experiences with Vipassana, Ayahuasca, Zen (and again, more) there is so much insight and wisdom to be gained within these pages.

Perhaps most importantly are a number of realistic and accessible pointers, suggestions, and practices that will help you form a legitimate understanding of what awaking, enlightenment, and direct experience really are. *Buddha On A Bull* is much needed read—now more than ever.

In Spirited Mischief and Love,

Chris Grosso,

author of *Indie Spiritualist, Everything Mind, and Dead Set On Living*

July, 2019

FOREWORD BY NURIT OREN AND GABOR HARSANYI

Do you believe in love at first sight?

That's how Gabor and I felt when we saw Elena and her partner, Anthony, in Budapest, Hungary, for the first time -- a tangible feeling of kinship and recognition. Needless to say, I was curious to read what Elena has written in her book.

The genuine, deep, charismatic and loving being that we met in the coffee shop was reflected perfectly in the pages of her book, in words that demonstrates a life not steeped in separation. With Elena, what you see is what you get. With Elena's book, what you read is what you get when you see Elena.

Our current spiritual arena is overflowing with teachings, modalities and concepts that are so easily available and that provide an endless source of satisfying group engagements and a myriad of opportunities for enhancing one's spiritual image. As easy as it is to be lost in a setting of "group think" and group pressure, it is indeed rare to find a seeker so sincere, deep and self-aware as Elena. This is demonstrated time and again throughout her book, as she stands naked before us, revealing both subtle and dramatic highs and lows of her well-travelled journey.

Here is a being who is humble enough to follow a teaching, a teacher or a modality that feels right and, at the same time, has the keen eye to see through spiritual bullshit and reject confusing, useless and false concepts and practices. She also displays the rare gift of courage — the courage it often takes to leave a group or a forum with detachment and without the kind of false loyalty that so often keeps a seeker enslaved and addicted to a path and its community.

As you read through these wonderfully descriptive pages, you can't help but find that Elena is no one's spiritual captive. Her complete freedom from the "keeping up with the spiritual Jones" type of peer pressure comes through very clearly, as she exhibits a result-oriented demeanor of one who stays tenaciously focused on the bottom line.

Gabor and I were so delighted to find that Elena shared in this book a question of vital importance: "How many people got enlightened through the method you are practicing?"

This is a significant point that Elena brings out in this book. There are many famous teachers today who have great credentials and who are surrounded by huge crowds, yet so few ever inquire how many of their students have actually awakened.

It is so easy to get high and fascinated, to have great "aha moments" and realizations, and to get stuck in the belief that someone outside of ourselves is "transmitting" something to us — all of which enhance the addiction to searching "out there", which is the number one enemy for one who wishes to stop the delusion and merry go round of mind-based spirituality and find lasting inner Silence.

Another essential ingredient in this book is Elena's sincere and open narration of her suffering. Many believe that once one is on a path to God there is nothing but grace and all should be smooth sailing. When this does not seem to be the case, we often feel that we must be doing something wrong. Of course, this is not true, any more than the belief that one must suffer to find Truth. Nonetheless, regardless of our beliefs, life happens, and the road can get pretty rough. Here is where Elena shines once again, using her pain and seeming misfortunes to drive her deeper and deeper into Being and to allow the essence of existence to burst forth as the powerhouse she has become.

Thank you, Elena, for opening your heart and sharing your amazing life. May this book bless anyone who delves into its evident and hidden treasures and makes them his or her own.

With love and appreciation,

Nurit Oren, author

with Gabor Harsanyi, author & Awakening Master

www.gaborharsanyi.com

INTRODUCTION

Do you think, dream, and desire to wake up? Do you feel, however, that awakening and enlightenment are rare phenomena and not attainable? Or, after many years of spiritual seeking, do you not believe that enlightenment is possible at all? Maybe you are confused about what awakening and enlightenment are. Do they actually exist?

All these questions were mine, too. I had no idea what "awakening" was and I wasn't sure "enlightenment" was possible. If it did exist, I wondered if it was only for a chosen few. The whole endeavor to become *enlightened* was very confusing, and yet for years it had a grip on me, like an annoying fly that won't leave when you are trying to relax at the beach. As much as I tried to brush it off, I couldn't just set it aside and forget it. As the fly leaves you alone only for a second just to try to land on you from another angle, the drive for enlightenment was relentless; it didn't spare me a peaceful moment!

This book is about how that drive got fulfilled. It is a story about awakening to who I am, about what I found enlightenment to be, and about what awaits the seeker when the seeking journey ends.

This book intends to open the reader to the very real possibility of awakening.

This book is *not* intended to set me up as a teacher. The teacher-student relationship inevitably creates duality. It creates a situation where one person *knows* and another person *wants to know*. Since my intention is to transmit the truth, the last thing I want is for you to take on the role of *someone who doesn't know*. The thinking mind may very well not know, but the deepest part of you knows it all.

The thinking mind is simply unaware of the truth of who you are. My deepest intention is for this book to remind you of that truth by facilitating within you moments of deep insight where the knowing of who you are may be revealed.

In this book, I use many stories from my own life and from the lives of people I know. Through these stories, commentaries, and direct guidance, I aim to point the mind in a direction that facilitates the experience of awakening.

The book has two main parts:

The first part is my story of awakening. This is intended for anyone curious about how it happened. But you'll soon see that it was not my main motivation for including it. If you just allow yourself to relax as the mind follows the story, the mind's resistance lessens, and this becomes a very potent time for unexpected, immediate, and sudden insight.

The second part is for the seeker who wants to wake up. Here again, you will find short stories that may facilitate deep insight. Most importantly, though, this is a simple *practical* map that can facilitate the enlightenment experience to wake you up to the truth of who you are. This map can be used to orient yourself, to recognize what keeps you from awakening now, so you can start right where you are. It encourages you to look at these obstacles using tools that are available to you right now, and to dive in with deep inquiry, and with no more delays.

Lastly, this book is written for you to *enjoy* reading. Even if enjoyment is all you gain from reading this book, it will still be worth my efforts.

"The big question is whether you are going to be able to say a hearty yes to your adventure."

Joseph Campbell

PART 1.

The End of the
Search: My Story
and Reflections.

CHAPTER 1.

The Nature of the Spiritual Search

1.1 THE UNCEASING SEARCH

If you asked me, "Was it worth it?" I would tell you without a second of delay: the lifelong search for the truth of who I am, regardless of how difficult it was, regardless of who and what I lost on the way, was worth every bit of life I lived, every bit of suffering I endured. It was worth everything that led to that very moment when who I am, what this life is about, what this world is about, was revealed.

The revelation is worth a human life. In fact, *enlightenment* happens when the human we think we are dies in that revelation and who we truly are is revealed. That moment—the knowing that comes from it—is worth the lifelong search. And if you believe in reincarnation, it is worth all the lifetimes it took to find the truth of being.

We seek that truth in so many ways and some of us get so close to the resolution of the search that it starts haunting us day and night without relief. Many of the mystics of the past tasted that constant yearning for truth without any resolution for years, decades, and lifetimes. At times the constant pain of separation from the truth of who we are, and the yearning for it, are unbearable. At other times it's exhilarating.

From the unbearable pain, mystics have written poems of deep suffering and great longing to meet with God, to merge with the Divine. From these moments of exhilaration have come songs of the merging of the divine lovers, or of finding solace in the hands of the Beloved.

And yet there is something—an awakened knowing, a realization of Truth—that is beyond even the highest intoxication from the experience of merging into divine union. This is why the mystic never relaxes; he/she either yearns for the merging

2

or is in a celebration of the union, and when that comes to an end, she is yearning again. This cycle is experienced again and again until Truth finally reveals itself and the search ends. Then she sings, because she loves to sing.

1.2 LIFESPAN OF THE SEARCH

In these times, so many of us long for—and feel ready for—enlightenment, but most of us are still seeking it without relief. Some people claim to have "called off the search". And then there are teachers who advise: "Don't call off the search prematurely."

There is no truth in either of these beliefs— that one can stop the search on demand or that it's possible to do so prematurely.

It's nonsense really, for if it truly is *you* who can decide to stop or not to stop the search, then most people on a path would have abandoned it by this time. Spiritual seeking is a very hard undertaking that requires much energy, attention, focus, time and even money. It basically rules one's life. Once it has begun it's really no longer up to the ego or I to decide if or when to stop.

The search starts and stops by itself. When I read the book, *In Search of the Miraculous* by P.D. Ouspensky, 20 years ago, I didn't think "I will start the search now." It just started. This book set me up for a lifelong search. I have met so many people whose search started with it. I also met someone who was furious that he'd read that book 15 years ago; he felt that it ruined his life. He was probably exaggerating to make a point, but he said that he was very tired from the constant longing to know the truth. He wanted to relax and just live. Of course, it is not the individual who decides to start and stop the search. Then who or what is it? What starts the search? What makes us step onto a path of seeking?

We live as though we are separate from everything that surrounds us. It is an illusion created by the conditioned mind. We don't know it's an illusion, but we feel something is not quite right, nevertheless. The truth is absolutely hidden from us—but it is there. And it gives us a nagging sense of dissatisfaction. We feel this dissatisfaction in relation to our life: it may arise in the form of a belief that we are *not good enough* and need to improve, or that there is more to life than what we are living. Sooner or later the sense of dissatisfaction comes to most of us in a myriad of ways, regardless of how well our life appears to be going from the outside.

In Buddhism, this nagging sense of dissatisfaction is called the *human condition*, which is the belief in a separate *me* and living accordingly. Ultimately, dissatisfaction can bring us to a book, a teacher, an event in life—something that sets us on a path of seeking for that hidden truth we don't even know exists. As soon as we step onto a path of seeking it, we are in up to our eyeballs. More and more hidden truths open to us with every turn of the path and we are unable to go back to innocent ignorance anymore. The main truth, however, remains hidden because to find it, the seeker himself has to vanish. There really is no way out of seeking except to keep seeking until, by grace, the Truth comes forth. Then the search stops by itself.

CHAPTER 2.

The seeker's Train

2.1 IN FOR A RIDE

A book, an event, however one first encounters the path, there really is no longer a choice whether to stop the search or to continue. Once you're in, you're in. And what you are in for is a ride on a seeker's path in a seeker's train. At times you start to suspect that the train is going in circles. Every time you feel you can get off at this stop or that one and finally become enlightened, the train continues on without even slowing down. I got onto the train with a book and stayed for many years, moving from car to car in my search.

I remember what I felt: after nine years or so of seeking, first for peace of mind, then for *mind purification* (as meditation was presented to me), I started to long for enlightenment. Not all of us are looking for enlightenment beginning with our first meditation; most of us are seeking resolution of personal dissatisfaction. When my seeking turned toward enlightenment, I felt a sense of urgency, a sense of standing on the edge, almost pressed against the wall: as I believed it at the time, the last wall between me and enlightenment. There was a strong feeling of duality active in my mind: *here I am, a seeker,* and *out there is enlightenment* that can happen in a future, and these somehow needed to be united. I felt as if my brain and my body would explode if I didn't get off that edge, or *penetrate that wall and merge with enlightenment.* This was the closest the mind could get to a visceral feeling and a description. Believe me, I wanted to end the search right there because it felt excruciating. But the seeker's train was going full speed and, locked into the ride, I started to think and live the "What is enlightenment?" question 24 hours a day, 7 days a week.

At one of the retreats I attended at the time, the words of S.N. Goenka, the Vipassana meditation guru, finally reached me: "The path is long. Step by step, step by step, lifetime after lifetime, we go toward enlightenment, but the path starts with a first step." "What?! What?!!" I yelled inside my own head. "After all these years of torturing myself in long meditations, totally devoted to this method, putting everything else on hold, wholeheartedly focusing my attention only on this meditation, it is not leading to enlightenment in this lifetime? It is ONLY a first step??!! Noooo! Fuck it. I can't do it anymore!" This is an exaggerated description of my response, but it had so much energy in it that I was able to shift my attention to what else might be around.

I started to go into different cars on that seeker's train and ask anyone I met, "What is enlightenment?" and "Is it possible in this lifetime?"

2.2 THE GURDJIEFF WAY: SELF-OBSERVATION

Message: Teachers are there to point, not to be attached to.

The very first car I ever boarded on the seeke'r train was the Gurdjieff Way. I hopped on it the day I opened the book *In Search of the Miraculous* in 1998.

I had a teacher, a friend, who gave me that book in the elevator of Time Inc., a big publishing corporation that occupied a whole high-rise building on 6th Avenue and 44th Street in Manhattan. A senior teacher in the Gurdjieff Way Foundation, Doug Spitz, was on its Board of Trustees and he was also my boss at Time Inc., where I worked as a Systems Analyst at the time. We spent years together in that car on the seeker's train, going over Gurdjieff's elaborate ideas from his book series called *All and Everything*. But mostly I learned *remembering myself*, or self-observation, which means being actively aware and mindful in every moment. This is the main idea for beginners with the Gurdjieff Way.

We think we know ourselves when in reality we don't even notice when we scratch our head. We may walk ten blocks and only when we arrive at our destination notice we are there. We act habitually, automatically, and don't even know it. We have so many roles, yet we are under the impression that each is us. We never see our authentic face, hidden as it is by the variety of masks we wear. We just get so engrossed in thinking—the story that goes on in our head—that everything else goes unnoticed.

I was striving to remember myself, to be mindful "breath by breath," as my teacher said was possible, only to arrive at the conclusion that I was helpless. I kept forgetting to observe myself drifting in activities and would notice sometime later that I'd forgotten. After practicing year after year, the forgetfulness periods became less and less frequent. But one day Doug ended up in an automobile accident and I realized that from then on, I was alone in that train car. I was devastated. At the time, I felt as if he held the keys to the wisdom and without him, I would be just lost. It turned out to be a lesson in non-attachment, a lesson not to rely on a teacher to hold my hand and sit with me until the final destination. Teachers have their own journeys and they are not necessarily next to us in the same coach for the duration of our travels. In the couple of weeks following Doug's death I sorted through all our emails and made a little book of his writings. Then I left.

2.3 ZEN: FAST TRACK TO STILLNESS

Message: The well-known path is not necessarily my path.

I tried the Zen car next door. It was all black and orderly and for the short time in it, I was hit several times with a wooden stick because I couldn't sit straight all day.

I ended up in a Zen Mountain Monastery one evening by mistake. I had signed up for an introductory weekend and mixed up the dates, arriving a week too early. The monastery was in the middle of *sesshin* -- a serious practice week for monastics and lay practitioners. I had never really done any serious meditation, besides occasional fifteen minutes in the morning, which is why I signed up for the introductory workshop, hoping to learn. It was in the middle of winter and I had driven for several hours from New York City to upstate New York, where the Zen Monastery was located. I arrived right before the sun started to set.

The place was a former Christian monastery, an old solid stone building in the forest. I knocked on the thick wooden door. After a while, it opened slightly and with a squeak. A surprised-looking man in black robes looked at me through the crack. With much enthusiasm, I told him I was there for the weekend. "I paid online!" I exclaimed, stressing this as if it was a secret code. In those years, most people would call a retreat center to register. The man in robes told me the workshop was the following week and closed the door. I was in disbelief. I surely didn't want to drive back several hours into the night. I knocked again. He opened the door and looked at me severely with a strong *NO* on his face. By this point I realized that I had, in fact, arrived a week early for the workshop but, with the arrogance of a novice, I told him straight up, "If I am here, I am supposed to be here!" He simply closed the door. I knocked again, and when he opened, told him I was not going anywhere and that I would sit on the steps until they allowed me to enter.

I remembered Zen stories I had read about the seeker who arrives at the monastery only to have the monks deliberately make him wait on the steps, testing his seriousness. So, I got really serious and decided that I wouldn't move, I would sit on the stone steps in the snow until they gave up and let me in. After a few more times of opening and closing the doors, the man in black robes allowed me inside to sit on a little stool and wait for the Abbott's decision. He tried to scare me away with his description of what sesshin really is and how impossible it is for a newcomer to follow the rigorous schedule. By that time, I had already made my decision so nothing would scare me away. After an hour of sitting on that stool and waiting, I ended up in the middle of a big dark hall with about 50 people dressed all in black and sitting motionless on black cushions. The meditation cushion I brought with me was dark blue, so they didn't allow it. I received a meditation bench upholstered with a black material.

"Whack!" "Whack!" I heard the sound of a wooden stick landing on people's shoulders in the dark. They use the long wooden stick to wake people up if they fall asleep or slouch. It actually feels pretty good when you know what's going on, but the sound of that stick in the dark wasn't anything I knew from the civilized world and with trepidation, I waited for the figure in the dark to approach me with a stick! Let me tell you, it was excruciatingly difficult to go through that week. I wanted to run away several times but there was a huge metal gate across the road that headed out of the monastery and it was locked. I checked it several times on my walks outside, my mind planning an escape, but I didn't have the guts to ask the monks to open it for me after I had stormed in there in the first place!

Eventually the week was over, ending my speedy introduction to serious Zen. I surely learned some stillness, regardless of the discomfort. I tested my survival limits, too! In the end I didn't like it, but mostly because of the constant bowing to Buddha. I just never got this shtick—not in the Zen monastery, not in the Russian Orthodox Church with all the bowing to Jesus. I learned that even a well-known spiritual path, like Zen, might not be my own path. I left the Zen seeker's car and never went back.

2.4 VIPASSANA: PURIFICATION OF THE MIND

Message: Engage in practice, but beware of blind reliance on methods.

Eventually I came across the Vipassana car and the beautiful, deep silence there. No guy with a stick, no bowing, no bells, no cymbals or other instruments being constantly hit in the middle of a Zen meditation to wake you up. You could build yourself a throne from the cushions, all colors and shapes; you just made yourself comfortable to sit still for l-o-o-o-n-g periods.

I became so blindly devoted to Vipassana meditation, mostly to the profound silence in sittings, that I didn't look for anything else. I closed my eyes in my first meditation and that was it. I didn't diverge even an inch from the instructions; I thought that anyone who did could not be a really serious meditator and I didn't have respect for that. I was a hardcore, intense seeker and I glued myself onto that cushion in the Vipassana coach.

I regularly attended Vipassana retreats in the tradition of S.N. Goenka, who taught the method of *purification of the mind* through awareness and equanimity with body sensations. I sat wholeheartedly for years, my eyes shut and my body motionless, trying to allow the body stillness to accommodate constant purification of the mind. Later I understood that the seeker's ego always finds an excuse to keep its identity. The seeker thinks he needs to purify the mind in order to attain enlightenment, whereas true enlightenment is the revelation of the very nature of the mind as empty. It turns out that the very common, strongly ingrained belief (formed in childhood) that we are not good enough affects the realm of spirituality as well; we try to fix ourselves, whether through therapy or meditation.

In Vipassana meditation, I sat through almost all the physical sensations a human being can experience in this life: benign feelings of the air touching my skin, distinct sensations of my body on fire, my legs falling asleep as though they were atrophying, pins and needles, the creepy-crawly sensations of wanting to jump out of my skin, and many, many more! I sat through the array of physical and mental pains until they would break down and completely disappear. I had many profound experiences, one after the other, tasting many mystical mind states. And yet, outside of the experiences, I was still under the impression that I was this hard-core seeker reaching for enlightenment.

It often happens that we get a new, even stronger identity from an activity with which we are deeply involved: in this case the activity of seeking. By sitting and observing firsthand, I learned impermanence, *anicca* in the ancient Pali language. I knew from my years in meditation that all phenomena are intrinsically impermanent. Everything—including all body and mind phenomena—arises and passes away. Except the Seeker. This dude was permanent.

I kept sitting and as I went deeper and deeper in meditation, I started to feel more and more disinterested in purifying the mind. I saw by this time the *bottomless bottom*: the more purification happens, the more there is still waiting to be purified! Suddenly my attention switched to the question of the possibility of enlightenment. I read about *sudden enlightenment* somewhere among my many spiritual books and I began to ponder whether it was possible in this lifetime. Was it possible for me? And one day I finally heard the voice of Mr. Goenka from the speakers mounted above my head in the meditation hall: "This is a first step ...step by step... for lifetimes." My utter disappointment in a method that suggested lifetimes of "purification" made me finally exit the Vipassana car.

Towards the end of my ride on the seeker's train I got really promiscuous, going from one car to another, bypassing many of them without stopping, or dropping in to visit without hanging out too long, bringing with me the same question: "What is enlightenment?"

2.5 JED MCKENNA: UNCOMPROMISING HONESTY

Message: Whatever the method, the main ingredient in spiritual awakening is bare honesty.

I met Jed McKenna in one of the cars. He was hiding from everybody, but he had a store set up full of books entitled *Spiritual Enlightenment: The Damnedest Thing* and two more with similarly provocative titles. People didn't know who this fellow Jed was, whether that was his real name, or whether he was even a real person. Nonetheless, I saw people with his books all over that coach, forgetting about their usual spiritual routines like morning

25

and evening meditations, advanced yoga classes, silent retreats, and weekly satsangs. They were all quietly reading his books and those who finished would leave the coach immediately, some leaving the seeker's train altogether.

This made me very curious. I bought a book, sat there in the corner and read. WOW. What a bold delivery of truth! I was totally hooked. It was fresh, engaging, and cut through New Age spiritual concepts and terminology I'd come to view as "bullshit." It was absolute dynamite; I felt a resonance in my bones. Something in me started to crumble. With profound honesty, Jed McKenna spoke to me through his series of books debunking enlightenment and he demanded the same in return. He painted a picture for me of a spiritual marketplace, just like a business marketplace, where everybody tries to sell their products and services, except that the product in a spiritual marketplace is enlightenment and the service is teaching a particular method of how to get there.

He asked me a question I had never asked anyone: "How many people got enlightened through the method you are practicing?" Without much pondering, my answer was simple: "None, as far as I know." I had never even thought of asking a question like that before; I would have seen it as arrogant. But not anymore. I took Jed McKenna's approach to heart as I left that car quickly and moved along the train, a seeker with a new attitude: "That's right, Jed, we are in a spiritual marketplace; let's get right to the 'bottom line'!"

2.6 AYAHUASCA: EXPLORATION OF ALTERED STATES

Message: Altered states in themselves have nothing to do with awakening.

This was one car I visited several times. Typically, I would return to it exhausted from seeking using another method or discipline. I would return to the *ayahuasca* car as one would visit a dining car on a passenger train. I secretly wished for a shortcut where I could drink a magic potion and suddenly become enlightened!

Usually you enter this coach by an invitation to a ceremony. Someone knows someone in the coach who can open the door and you buy a ticket for a ride through the night. I got in for the first time in the year 1999 for a ceremony with a man who called himself a *techno shaman* and his co-facilitator, a woman psychotherapist. The techno shaman was a young man who also used different bio-feedback devices to calm the mind. He was great at mixing music and *icaros*, songs of the ayahuasca shamans of the Amazon.

On this first visit that took place in a teepee on a private property in upstate New York, I had a shot of *ayahuasca* tea, the mind-altering substance from the Amazon rainforest. I was completely overtaken by the medicine. I laughed, cried, made violent noises, vomited into a bucket, traveled to different realities in my own mind, danced, got horny, felt the universal love, and rode an imaginary horse with every molecule of my body to the rhythms of the icaros. This visit was so packed with experiences that by the morning I was completely exhausted and glad that the horse had finally left me alone so that I could sleep for a couple of hours without any movement!

Later in the morning there was a sharing circle and everyone else was ready to dive into the experience again the following night. They all had a two-day ticket. They described the ride as a mind-altering magical journey. As wondrous as it was for me as well, I really wasn't as impressed as everyone else. I was still there, near my bucket, in the same skin, unenlightened!

Over the years, when I visited the ayahuasca car for a night, I would see a lot of new people and some old timers too; they would still be there, a decade later, with their bucket. On these visits, the train would go through the Andes Mountains in Peru, where I would be given a freshly made light-green tea from the San Pedro cactus that grows abundantly in that area; or the train would go through the

Amazon Forest in Ecuador, where I would be served a familiar thick dark ayahuasca brew; or it would run somewhere in quiet suburban area of USA, or even someone's city apartment, with an offering of illegally transported South American brew or home-made tea from internet-bought dried vine. Always, the tea was served together with a bucket—which I would find useful every time!

As anyone familiar with medicinal plant substances knows, they are powerful healers. I have much respect for medicinal substances. It is still a mystery to me how a plant communes with a human to make this journey together. During those communions I had many insights. I would lose anxieties and certain fears; some contradictions in my psyche would be resolved. Every time I took the medicine, I would feel wiser, more open, more peaceful, more alive, more loving, more empowered, healthier, more radiant. There was always some change. But my search for enlightenment would continue with more zest and renewed effort, since the expanded states were definitely more alluring than everyday mind states. My main inquiry "What is enlightenment?" remained unanswered.

With time, I started to realize that altered states themselves have nothing to do with awakening or enlightenment. They can help in showing an endless variety of possible mental states, all of which are transitory in nature. Everyday mind states vary just as much as those induced by psychedelics. We are in a perpetual trip that the mind takes us on, right from the day we identify with the human character we call *I*. Altered states of mind, as alluring and wondrous as they may be, are all part of the overall dream state of being identified with a dream character.

2.7 ABRAHAM HICKS: OBSERVATION OF THOUGHTS

Message: Be open; insights on how to proceed can come in unorthodox ways.

By this time, I was open to anything, anything that might work, and I went so far as to visit a car with Esther and Jerry Hicks. I talked in a channeled session with some non-physical entities who called themselves Abraham. No kidding!

I raised my hand in an auditorium full of overly joyful people who asked Abraham how to manifest a dream house or a dream job. The only question I could press out of my tense mouth was: "What is enlightenment?"

Esther listened to me intently and then started to talk. I felt a kind of buzz in the body and entered a hypnotic state. I was fixed on the image of Esther in front of me and Esther/Abraham was explaining how humans love to get themselves deep down into a rabbit hole and then dig themselves out, celebrating victory at the end. They were saying that to get enlightened one doesn't need to dig oneself into the hole but instead connect and align with the Higher Self. I was okay with Esther/Abraham making their point, using me as an example of a hard-headed human who likes to suffer.

I continued to sit and drift in my hypnotic state while Esther/Abraham compared a toaster to the *lower self* and electricity to the *higher self*, and talked about connecting the toaster to the electricity by plugging the cord into the socket. I know this analogy works for many, but it didn't work for me. I wasn't about to settle for a dualistic view of lower and higher selves. I had years of deep insights from my meditation practice by this time and knew that the material world is an illusion and duality is only a perception. The whole interaction only made me more confused, even somewhat angry, and so, as they said, I went deeper into the hole I was digging.

The Abraham teaching went beyond the words, as I found out later; the interaction produced in me some kind of vertigo state in which I was unable to walk out of the door thinking any negative thought. As soon as any came up, I would feel nauseous and lightheaded. This uncanny health issue brought my attention to thoughts. If in Vipassana my attention was mostly on sensations, now all my attention was on thoughts. What are they? How do they originate? What exists in between thoughts? What makes us think particular thoughts? Do we have a choice in thinking? Can we stop thinking? Because of this mysterious vertigo that occurred after "talking" to Abraham, I was forced to be vigilant and focused and to notice every thought. I still don't know who Abraham really is or what happened to me, but I was definitely pointed to look into an area that was previously a bit vague, to clarify the relationship between sensations, feelings, and thoughts. To this day, I still call Esther/Abraham *Abrahamchiki*, which in Russian suggests they are more than one and also adds a certain softness to their name.

2.8 ADYASHANTI: AWAKENING

Message: Awakening to Awareness is not the end of the search.

Next, I stumbled upon the biggest car of the train: 300 passengers sat at a week-long retreat with the Zen drop-out leader, Adyashanti. I paid my dues and joined the retreat. It was August 2009 at the Omega Institute in upstate New York.

Adyashanti was a charismatic, clear-talking guy who showed respect for my long involvement with Vipassana meditation, just as I respected his years in Zen. I guess we need some hard-earned credentials and some commonality to trust a teacher. Since I myself was a dropout, and to me,

Adyashanti's 15 years in Zen served as evidence of reliable effort, I could trust his guidance.

He guided me to shift the focus out from feelings and sensations in meditation (my training from years in Vipassana) and to "zoom out" rather than "zoom in." Adyashanti calls his method *natural meditation*. It is based on the Zen method of *shikantaza*—just sitting.

One of the first meditations resulted in *satori*, one of the classic awakening experiences: a sudden experience of oneness, where focus and identification as a separate self suddenly loosened and shifted instead to pure Awareness. I spent the rest of the retreat walking around *as Awareness*, marveling at the oneness of the world. I would live in that state for the rest of my life if possible, but the world contracted into *me, Elena* very soon after I returned home from the retreat. My neighbor had a major construction project going on right in front of my house and the noises all day long loudly called me back to the seeker's train. It took a little while for the hammer and the drill to get me back there—but sure enough, there I was: "Hey, guys, I'm back! How's the ride going?" In truth, I had never really gotten off the train; it had just felt like that for a week or so!

While I've described it in a light-hearted way, to put this experience of awakening into the right perspective, I would have to say that awakening is nothing less than a profound shift of attention. Suddenly attention shifts from the character we think we are to pure Awareness. It is almost a reversal of a foreground (self, me) and a background (pure Awareness, presence—any name you can give to the full expansion and release from the focus on *me*).

If you have ever played with adjusting the focus of a camera you will understand this analogy. You set the focus on the person in the shot and you get the crystal-clear picture of the person with a blurry background behind. When you set the focus on the background, the person fades and whatever was in the background now becomes crystal clear. The same phenomenon occurs with awakening. For a second or longer, the mind's contraction into the character relaxes, making the background of pure Awareness alive and *the person* fades. Even for a short time, the mystery opens itself and now it is clear that *the character "you"* is not a true identity, but simply the one you are mostly used to.

When you come back from the experience, whether only a second or hours later, there is a memory of the experience which the mind will immediately label as something that happened to *me, the seeker*. It will also try to own the experience in a more grandiose way: *I am Awareness*. Still, awakening is an important event on a seeker's path: now you definitely know you are not only this body, this character. Now you might believe you are

Awareness, but this belief is not really sustainable because it only comes from the memory of the event, which is conceptual thinking. In fact, in many people an awakening experience kickstarts the search. Many people nowadays, not just traditional spiritual seekers but people living regular lives, experience sudden awakening. No striving for truth, no meditation for years—nothing like that. "I went to the forest, a pinecone fell on my head, boom— awakening!" I heard a story of a biker who had a road accident. While he was flying through the air and before he hit the ground, he experienced awakening. You come back from the experience to your regular life with a changed perception. You can't live anymore as before. Now you have many questions. You won't stop asking until you find out who you really are, and the search comes to an end all by itself.

CHAPTER 3.

Enlightenment

3.1 THE GATELESS GATE

I left the train when the train disappeared— and me too! One evening by the fireplace in my own living room, in an online inquiry guided by a 19-year-old, I realized that I do not exist.

It was October 2010. My guide's name was Unison; he was a member of what became an infamous online forum called *Ruthless Truth*, intended to point people to no-self insight. Their process worked miraculously for some seekers who were willing to receive the fire of several angry men at once yelling at them: "Look! There is no you, motherfucka!"

Apparently, such unexpected language and fire jolted seekers into unfamiliar territory where their achievements in life and in spiritual practice were "not worth an eaten egg," as we say in Russia. It would cause them to drop their usual thinking and at that very potent moment they would be struck with the offering: "You do not exist." This would produce a mind state of *no self, selflessness*, where they could see that what they thought they were—a separate person, me—they were not!

Unison was a bit different from everybody else on this forum. I liked his name and his gentleness; he was the only one who didn't curse, or perhaps he just cursed the least. He was the age of my own son. He was a college student and worked too, so he could only work with me at night. On this particular night, I set myself up in my living room, having made sure my family had gone to sleep.

All day prior to this night, I had felt an intensity in the air. I was completely fixated on how to penetrate this enlightenment. I thought I might die, disappear, or just go crazy. These thoughts brought with them fear, even terror. After a while the terror changed into a deep sadness, almost as if I was grieving for someone. I felt this deep sadness in every cell, every molecule of my body.

The decision came by itself ultimately, arising from the depths of my being. I stood in my kitchen, the decision to do this inquiry and to dive into the unknown felt so strongly that I had to hold onto the counter. I felt lightheaded but as the decision came, I made a step forward, let go of the counter and there I was: at the Gateless Gate.

For centuries, this Gate has attracted seekers of truth. It is the final frontier: the only entry through it is to lose the seeker itself. The seeker can't go through the Gate; the seeker has to die. What is left after the seeker dies is Life itself and the Gate is seen to be gate-less. In reality the Gate does not exist; there is no one crossing the Gate, and there is no crossing either, just a shift in perception of what one is.

Unison instructed me to look at any object without assigning a word to it. I was looking at the burning logs in the fireplace and tracking exactly what I was seeing and feeling. Suddenly, I realized that *log* was just a label for an event that was happening. If I didn't know the word for log, I would just be experiencing the log as small children experience the world, not knowing words or labels yet. As soon as I saw the log as an experience, rather than a thing, everything else became an experience, a movement in consciousness—including me. *Me* was seen to be a concept, a mere concept that the mind had held for so long that it had become reality. It wasn't real, just like Santa Claus isn't real, but we live in the grand illusion that he is.

As a child you may believe in *Santa*: the one who brings you presents under the Christmas tree. And then one day you see that it is your parents who secretly put the presents under the tree. Your friends who are already disillusioned by this age confirm it. The loss of innocence at first might be shocking, but then you just continue to play at the Santa story every Christmas, still receiving presents under the tree.

This is exactly what happened when I saw that *I* do not exist. *I* as a separate being, with a name, was seen as merely an illusion. I didn't die in the end, and I didn't disappear. The illusion is what is not real and it can't, therefore, die: it does not exist in the first place. What disappeared was the sense of self, the unconscious contraction into the character as though it were a real entity. Life itself showed up as aliveness in a variety of movements: as seeing, hearing, sensing, feeling, thinking, without anyone to actually own these activities.

I had had experiences of oneness before where I would suddenly find myself in a selfless state. After the experience was over, the *I* would reconstruct itself, immediately assuming ownership for the experience as if it had happened to *me*.

This is very common on the path when the seeker experiences any number and type of spiritual states, only then to come back to the perception of *me* having had the experience.

I am very grateful to my teacher Doug Spitz, who from the beginning told me: "States do not matter. Self-observation has more value than any of the spiritual states, though they are interesting." I didn't actively long for the special states, but there was likely a subtle attachment to them anyway. Without proper wisdom being present at the time, an individual coming back from such an experience typically interprets it as "I had an experience," therefore locking him/her into more seeking: trying to repeat, re-experience, make it happen again, which leads to feeling even more separation and more suffering. As Mr. Goenka said in his talks: "You want enlightenment so much that you run toward it with all your might, only going the opposite way, away from it."

In my room, in front of the fireplace, already deep into the night, I laughed, for this truth of oneness had been present all the time, but the self-hypnosis of being a separate me had totally distorted the reality! Seeing this clearly made me laugh: "Now I know why the mystics of all times called enlightenment a cosmic joke!" My beliefs had compartmentalized Life into separate objects and into a me to whom life was happening. Seeing separation as an illusion was just a shift in perception, nothing more. Surely a joke!

This experience of clarity obliterated the seeker's train, which was seen as external and separate from me—as a life I was living, a path I was walking. Now there was no separation between me and Life.

3.2 THE FREE FALL

After the evening with Unison, I found myself upside down, suspended in space, falling in no particular direction, not knowing who I was or where I was. The only thing I knew was: "*I* am not Elena, I am not separate, I am not thoughts, not feelings and not anything I thought I was before." Truly *I* was not. Who I was I didn't know, but already *this* felt much better than what was before: the claustrophobic train, the sense of separation, contracted into a body, brain, thoughts and feelings.

At that point, one might expect to quit the search, not being on the train anymore... But the seeker's path starts with a train, and proceeds with a free fall—and still there were some questions! The main question that arose was: "Who am I?"

As I experienced this question in me, more falling, more feeling lost and disoriented, more seeking arose. What was clear that *I* was only a construct, a belief, and that I really couldn't do anything, couldn't decide, choose, or stop. I could only *be*. The search would continue, and I could only *be*. I could no longer choose the train, the car, where to sit, what to think. Now I was simply experiencing this happening in me: thinking, breathing, living, falling. It was as if the temperature was rising in a body that I couldn't control, and there was only the experiencing of heat.

Shinzen Young, a Vipassana teacher I studied with online, describes this as "learning to live as the wave, instead of the particle." He compares the state of being after an enlightenment experience to learning to walk as a baby, constantly falling down, getting up and trying again. After experiencing awakening, we have to learn how to live again, almost backwards. We are able to walk and hold ourselves upright in a physical body, but we have to learn to live in a world as though we were *a person*, when we now know that we are not. Without the perceived boundaries of separation, life flows through us in an unimpeded wave, knocking over all the beliefs, concepts and artificially installed structures that we have been building all our lives, and now all those structures are falling. Everything we thought we were, we are not. Everything we thought we knew, we don't.

3.3 WHO AM I?

"Who am I?" This question was taking me for a ride—and a free fall! It kept swirling in my head, day and night. If I could, I would have quit at this point! The "What is enlightenment?" question didn't torture me anymore; it had morphed into an experience of the immediacy of life. In my experience there was no *gentle relaxation* into the next state of being. The fall was not a smooth glide. Instead, it brought along with it a collapse of all the structures: a fire in the house, a separation followed by divorce and, if those were not enough, loss of concentration and memory! The stress of the changes in my life was too big for my system. I had the sense of being completely disabled, almost as if I had had a selective lobotomy: I didn't remember how it had been before,

I didn't have much sense of time, I didn't remember what the day was, or even the year, and I didn't know how old I was or what exactly I was supposed to do in this life. I only remembered the question: "Who am I?" I started to look for a retreat just to have a break.

A Vipassana center that I knew was holding a 20-day silent retreat and would provide a room and board. I could go there and just *be*! There was one concern: the center had very strict requirements for long retreats and I could pass all of them except one: I was no longer used to sitting in formal meditation for at least 2 hours a day, every day. To me, *everything* was now meditation—there was no separation between me and Life. I went ahead and said "yes" to all the scrutinizing questions on the application form.

I had an interview there with the teacher I was closest to. Before signing my application, the teacher actually winked at me! I was not devoted to Vipassana meditation anymore, but she also knew something that somehow made her sign my application.

I learned later that this teacher didn't have long to live—she had cancer—and she knew I had to be in that retreat. She had seen me sitting, year after year, and she knew I was ready for whatever would transpire in that retreat. Her wink was her subtle way of telling me: "Don't worry: the rules do not matter. I know you and I am happy to be here to help."

I arrived at the retreat center, this time without any agenda: no more striving to achieve something in the meditation practice, just a chance to rest and be. I arrived there as if to my own home; it was so familiar to me. I felt held by my room, by some of the familiar people serving in the retreat's kitchen and office, and by the familiar schedule and restrictions (basically *no* to everything except unceasing Vipassana meditation all day every day).

Finally, I had a little more sense of being *grounded*:
I had my own room with a view, good food and 20
days of time for myself. I felt invited by the space and
by everything in me to relax and *be*.

Long retreats differ from the regular 10-day
retreats in the Vipassana center since no one really
watches you, what you do or how you do it. From
your application, the teacher's recommendation, and
your documented history in the center's database, it
is assumed that you: (a) have meditated two hours
a day regularly for at least five years, (b) are not
involved in any other technique of meditation or
"energy work," (c) have not had any alcohol for at
least two years, and (d) have arrived in motionless
daily meditations at a relative calm. There is a
schedule for these long retreats but it's almost
optional; you can more or less lead your own retreat.

I chose to sit in a cell—a space that looked like
a small closet, dark and soundproof. I sat and when I

couldn't sit, I walked in the forest. The same question was running in my head: "Who am I?"

The question was automatic. It arose without my conscious effort. I didn't even invite it; it felt as though it were just renting a space in my head.

As the hours and days went by, the question morphed into different variations depending on what I was experiencing. If I sat and experienced discomfort, the question became: "Who is experiencing discomfort?" If I walked in the forest and delighted in the fresh air opening my lungs, the question was: "Who is that, delighted?" If the thought came to me: "I wonder what time it is now," the question that would pop up next was: "Who is asking?" The question became like a self-winding mechanism. It soon simplified itself to: "Who was that just now?" At some point it even became funny, as the question would morph into: "And *seriously*, who was that?" This one produced an inner smile.

It almost became a game when the question would catch the tail of another thought and cut it off with the nonchalant: "Who the fuck is thinking?"

This inquiry continued around the clock, even in my sleep. I know this because a character in my dream would ask the same questions in her head and this would wake me up.

On Day 13 of the retreat I came out of the cell in the middle of the day and realized it was my birthday. "Happy birthday to me!" said the thought. "Whose birthday?" came the question.

I couldn't sit in the dark anymore, so for the following days I mostly walked in the forest, or lay in my room, or sat in the hall with others.

These next few days turned me into a mystic...

3.4 ENCHANTMENT

Falling deeper into silence, I experienced the incredible enchantment of the mystic. Walking in the forest, I would talk to God. I would sing to God (silently) as if I were the reincarnation of Hafiz, the 14th-century Persian poet that I admired. Well, maybe that's too much of a claim, but it surely felt like it! I would write mystic-like poems in a notebook:

> God is the best engineer, best architect, best artist, best actor!
>
> He molds himself into the blade of grass,
>
> the bird's chirp,
>
> the wind's whisper,
>
> the thought and heartbeat of a human being.

I see now where he hides!

That's him, rejoicing and smiling now!

What a delightful meeting!

Or I would write aphoristically:

Fall in love with silence rather than thinking.

Thinking will draw your attention,

Like a flashy, promiscuous dancer.

Marry silence.

"How can you *not* be, *not* here, *not* now?!" In my mind I would challenge Ram Dass, the famous teacher who wrote the book *Be Here Now*, as it became clear to me that I am always here and now, and only the thinking mind might hide this simple fact of existence.

"As long as you think you are *that*, you are not. You, that thinks, is an illusion." I would converse in my mind with Nisargadatta, the teacher of non-duality and author of the book called *I AM THAT*. I wasn't sure yet who or what I was, but I was certain he wasn't addressing the thinking mind in his title. So, we were in agreement on that.

Then I would write in metaphor:

"Complete silence and non-action for an extended period works like a Thai massage: it bends, squeezes, stretches, and presses you down. At first you are confused; then you are in agonizing pain; then you are paranoid that the therapist wants to break you; then you relax, surrender, and soften."

Or I would simply record the insights after walking in the forest:

"We overlook the essential. We take it for granted, because we never had an experience without this *essential* present. We fear dying but because we never really noticed the *essential*, we think, instead, that we are afraid of losing the body.

63

When my little kitten died in my hands, it was terrifying and fascinating to see his body be one moment animated, and the next moment lifeless. This *essential*—aliveness that permeates the body—is always here and therefore unnoticed. It's a given: we do not need to ask for it, work for it, pray for it. *I exist* is the simplest truth that one can realize in any given moment. It is prior to anything I can tell about myself. Before I am someone or somebody, I simply am: I exist."

The world around me, too, was responding to the enchantment in me and it organized events I couldn't explain. This only added to the mystery. I would start to see the numbers 4:44 on the clock in my room. This had never happened to me before. I was never *mystically inclined*. I have been an almost scientific investigator of the mind through methodical meditation. I was surprised to experience events I couldn't explain. I didn't try to be in my room for this *4:44 event*. I didn't have a watch; in a retreat, all activity goes by the sound of the gong. I would wake up between 4:00 and 4:30 a.m. to the gong, do my usual morning routine, suddenly glance at the clock, and it would read 4:44 a.m.! Or I would come to my room in the middle of the day, not knowing what time it was, even what day it was, and there it would be 4:44 p.m. on the clock.

Then there was the day I was sitting on a garden bench in the middle of a lawn. I had sat there so many times before on other retreats, but this day was different. I felt the closest to God I have ever felt. I felt that my body was some kind of an avatar for God to experience life in all the splendor of the senses: touching, seeing, hearing, tasting, sensing. I exclaimed internally, "This is a totally amazing, multidimensional, multi-sensory, absolutely fascinating, marvelously intricate, full-blown illusion of a world!" And I looked through the holes in my *avatar suit* onto this amazing world: the body, the grass, the trees, the sky... I was looking into the sky when I saw a flock of 20 ravens circling above me. It was an almost impossible scene. I had never seen so many birds in one place circling, almost covering the whole sky. In disbelief, I even counted them.

These events, though they do not hold much significance for me now, carried a mystical flair in them at the time, adding to the enchantment, expanding the mind toward limitlessness. This is a very beautiful place to be and some seekers just stop here and rest for a lifetime. I am almost jealous of this option, but I was in a search for the whole enchilada; I would not be able to stop seeking until arriving at full clarity, beyond a doubt, of who I am and what this life is about. It wasn't really my decision to continue: a certain momentum was carrying me along in this inquiry.

3.5 DEEP INSIGHTS, SILENCE

My mind was expanding in insight. I had
an experience one day while passing by the big
bathroom mirror on my way to the meditation hall.
Since there is not much to do on a long silent retreat
apart from sitting, you get very creative about how
to kill time when you can't sit, walk, or even sleep
anymore. You clean your room. The room is so
clean by the end of the retreat that the mirror does
not have a single streak on it to distort the images.
This particularly clean mirror suddenly reflected my
world in it so clearly that there was no separation
between the image and the surface of the mirror. The
next hour in the meditation hall I sat amused by the
illusory nature of the visual images in the mirror, as
though I was peeking into the whole unknown world.

Later, on the last day of the retreat, this came back to me as a perfect representation of the world we live in, of its illusory nature:

> "As the mirror holds the images without the images distorting the mirror, Consciousness holds this world of objects without them distorting the primordial container of Consciousness. They can't be separated; one does not exist without the other. What makes a mirror *a mirror* is the ability to produce and hold the images, and the image does not exist if there is no mirror. The two are inseparable."

I was dipping my toes in what Buddhism calls *Emptiness*, the realization of the illusory nature of the apparent world of phenomena.

During one meditation, I recalled a school theatre group I was in as a schoolgirl and how we fought to play the main characters, those that appeared most often on the stage, those with the most lines. The characters we wanted to play were often not even those that could be considered *positive*. I found myself talking in my head to someone, explaining this, but in reality, I was talking to myself: "Now there is a character, so-called 'you' (insert name), and suddenly there is a wish for it to be different, better, less complex, more *positive*. The wish happens only because you identified with this character so much that you forgot who you are and what is really going on. Wake up!"

During the last three days, my meditations became very, very quiet. The "Who am I?" automatic inquiry gave way to Huang Po's phrase: "Be still. Do nothing." Huang Po was an early Chinese Zen Buddhist master. His teachings were translated in a little book I read some time before and now he had come to point me to who I am:

"Perhaps you can concentrate your thoughts for a moment and avoid thinking in terms of good and evil. While you are not thinking in terms of good and evil, just at this very moment, return to what you were before your father and mother were born."

Huang Po had uncompromising teachings for me. Every time a thought arose, this phrase would arise too: "Be still. Do nothing." The thought would vanish. After a long period of "no-thought," one thought would crawl in very quietly and affirm: "Profound silence."

"Be still. Do nothing," Huang Po would say in my head.

3.6 THE GREAT SUFFERING

G.I. Gurdjieff, the great mystic of the beginning of the 20th century and teacher to many of the world's brightest minds, the one whose work I studied for the first several years of my search, believed in the value of suffering. He made a distinction between unconscious and conscious suffering. He even had a specific recipe for enlightenment with essential ingredients in it. Put together, these would make enlightenment a possible outcome, though not a guarantee. He presented the recipe as a combination of *intentional suffering* (deliberate acceptance of uncomfortable conditions) and *conscious effort* (self-observation, mindfulness). In his work he would create conditions in which students would feel great discomfort in

order to draw their attention away from thinking and
daydreaming and toward what was actually going
on in the body and mind. These conditions would
cause Gurdjieff's students to apply a conscious effort
of practicing self-remembering, mindfulness. "Live
a life of friction. Let yourself be disturbed as much
as possible, but observe," said Gurdjieff. "When no
emotions are aroused there is no friction, there is no
development."

By the end of the retreat I was living out these
conditions.

I was in the middle of an awful divorce, which
had been going on for two years. My house was a
total mess after the fire: no kitchen, no furniture, just
two mattresses in different rooms for my son and me,
and a table we made from our entrance door which
had been knocked out in the fire by the firefighters.
I covered the door with a waterproof tablecloth and
we put it on top of some wooden boxes in the center

of what had been the kitchen, turning them into a kitchen counter. The renovation workers connected a plastic utility sink and a stove for us so that we could make our meals. I knew I'd have to continue to renovate the house and sell it to complete the divorce. Since I had almost totally lost my ability to concentrate, I couldn't work.

My husband was now with another woman, who was pregnant. He was already thinking about how he would support another family. Even though I initiated the separation, I didn't know how I would support myself and how I would live without my husband, the house, and the life we had together for almost 14 years. I had to start my life again, but I wasn't young anymore and I wasn't well, health-wise. The doctors diagnosed me with autoimmune condition called Hashimoto's Disease. My loss of concentration was a result of that, they said. I tried to file for disability, but I was too disabled to follow up with appointments and the Disability Office dropped me. *Falling* at what seemed like the speed of light, I was a mess psychologically and was physically ill, too.

On Day19 of the retreat, I experienced something that resembled a panic attack. I had never experienced panic attacks before, but my husband was a psychiatrist and working with him in his office for many years had taught me the symptoms of many disorders. So, after all the profound silence I had experienced in the previous few days, there I was in my room, suddenly feeling such intense emotional pain that I just wanted to die! I wanted to quit. I didn't want to go through the divorce. I didn't want to see my husband with another woman. I didn't want to worry about my future. I just wanted to quit this pain that was absolutely unbearable.

The question "Who am I?" that had previously occupied my mind was gone. So too, were the enchantment, Huang Po, and all the profound stillness of the mind. There was only unbearable suffering, a sense of injustice, victimhood, disempowerment, anguish. I looked at the clock and there were my numbers: 4:44 p.m. "This really is a curse," I thought. I couldn't even cry; it was just too painful.

I decided to lie down and die. I wasn't thinking straight. I had regressed completely into being a victim of the circumstances. Lying down didn't bring relief. My body couldn't keep still; it was contracting. I wanted to die so much I contracted my body even more, hoping I could just disappear if I squeezed myself hard enough. As much as I tried to die, I couldn't. The level of suffering reached its peak, the contracting reached its limits, and still I was there, in the body, on the bed, exhausted.

"I can't die. Even if I want to, I can't. It's not me who decides when this character gets powered off," I finally was able to cry, "the freaking, fictional 'I' that feels so real!" Crying relaxed me a bit. In that little relaxation, I decided to stay for the final day in the retreat center. I knew that no one would give me the keys to my car before the retreat ended the next day without seriously questioning me about my reasons, and I was not interested in talking to anyone. So, I made a decision that made me feel complete in the moment:

"I will stay here today, and tomorrow I will leave the center and check myself into a psychiatric hospital." Yes! I had heard about "checking oneself into a psychiatric hospital" so many times in my husband's office. This idea sounded so perfect for me now! I repeated this phrase several times and it gave me a huge sense of relief. By that time, I felt no interest in enlightenment, who I am, the truth—any of it. I was just grateful for the break from suffering that arrived with the brilliant idea about the psychiatric hospital.

I almost fell asleep in that comfort, but then remembered that I had to go to the final meditation. I knew that if I didn't, the retreat assistants would come for me anyway. They would see I was not in the meditation hall and they would come and knock on my door.

I rose from my bed feeling calm. The storm had passed. I put my shawl on, opened the door and stepped outside.

3.7 I AM

When I had arrived at the retreat center, on the first day, I had immediately noticed a tree on the lawn in front of my room. It was a perfect tree, from its trunk to the almost symmetrical shape of its crown. There were other perfect trees, but this one really caught my attention. For no apparent reason, I just really liked the tree. And now, as I stepped outside, the tree was right in my face. It actively drew my attention to itself like a strong magnet. I stopped and looked.

All of a sudden, the tree started to lose its solidity that had been perceived before. It was morphing into a holographic *image of a tree* right in front of my eyes. When the tree completed its transformation, the space surrounding the tree continued to morph, as did the space beyond it. After the epic emotional catharsis in the room I had no energy left to even be surprised. I just stood there, motionless and neutral. In a split second the whole world morphed into a holographic image. I was gone.

I don't know how long this lasted, since there was no reference to time or space in that experience, only a translucent, holographic image that appeared instead of the world I knew.

My body was a part of this image but since there was nothing saying "I" or "this is me, mine," the body was just there, a part of the hologram. In one fell swoop, the whole world collapsed into a vision. There were no objects, only a holographic representation of them.

At some point, a feeling of fascination with the experience began to arise within the hologram, and this immediately transformed the body-hologram back into the human body. Now I was back in the body and everything folded back into the reality of sky, trees, grass, buildings.

I walked to the meditation hall. I entered the hall and sat down on a cushion. There were other people sitting in front of me. I was not interested in meditation anymore. "It doesn't work anyway" was the thought I heard in my mind. I was exhausted. I just needed to wait until the end of the retreat, to adhere to the schedule, and "all would be fine," I told myself mentally, guiding myself in this plan. I sat down on my cushion and looked right in front of me into the darkness of the meditation hall and at the motionless figures of my fellow meditators. Suddenly the space morphed again into a holographic image. The meditator me was gone.

The hologram this time was the image of the hall and meditators on cushions, including my own image. I was Buddha! There was a sudden recognition of *Primordially Pure Buddha Nature*, which is already *All* and *Everything* with no need to strive for it. What strives is the mind through its self-perpetuating story of needing to improve, achieve, attain perfection. It is all already perfect, and I am that perfection! Buddha itself! And each *person* who had been there just a moment before as a meditator was now Buddha. The life-world itself was Buddha! Inner laughter! Bwahahahaha!

"There are no people!"

"There is no path!"

"There is no goal!"

"There is no striving for Enlightenment!"

"There is no Enlightenment!"

"It's all an illusion!" Bwahahaha!

The inner laughter folded the hologram back into its own proper physical representation. I had an impulse to rise and storm out of the hall. And maybe even to yell: "Stop torturing yourselves! It doesn't matter! Go do something better than this with your lives!" And maybe even slam the door so they would wake up! Yes, wake up!

"Wake up!!" I yelled, but only internally. A feeling of compassion arose in me: "Sh-sh-sh." You know that situation when you walk through a room where people are sleeping and you don't want to wake them up, so you tiptoe through the room, carefully open the door and slowly close it so as not to disturb their sleep? That's exactly what I did.

I stepped outside, closing the heavy door behind me with extra care. It was already dark and the sky was lit with stars. The Vipassana center in Massachusetts is in the middle of nowhere and there are no artificial lights around, only stars. The moment was so magnificent. I stopped, looked at the dark ground, and then raised my eyes to the sky. The world collapsed once again.

The body was looking up to the sky in one holographic image. A little haiku poem voiced itself in it:

"From the furthest star

to the blade of grass

I AM"

Suddenly, welling up from within the hologram, was that question which had earlier turned into the self-perpetuating loop: "Who am I?"

The Voice answered with proper pauses, affirming each word:

"I AM.

One Mind.

Buddha.

God."

The voice-word *God* brought forth a sudden feeling of shame (probably from a trace of Russian

Orthodox Christianity with its focus on humility) and immediately this feeling folded the hologram back into the physical world, enlivening the senses. The fresh crisp evening air touched my skin. "Brrrr. Cold." I, now again the human, was standing there with eyes wide open, on a grass lawn, in the dark, with the starry sky above. I was filled with a silent, complete awe by the realization that there is no space, no time, no physical world. Only *I AM*.

"Be still

and Know.

I AM.

God."

Huang Po spoke in my mind with affirming authority.

The next day the retreat was over. This was my last day of seeking. The search stopped. Life continued.

AFTERWORD TO PART 1

I didn't have any point of reference for this experience: I had never read about, nor been told of, such an experience. I didn't have an explanation for it, I talked to no one about it and if I tried, it was reduced to a description that did not approach what I was left with. I knew that it was *Revelation* with a capital R; it completely shed all doubts and subtle striving to know, erasing all questions. It was *Knowing* itself and what was presented in that *Knowing* was life—the simple, ordinary life of a sentient being which continues in spite of this *Revelation*. I am not and yet I am. The world we live in is not and yet it is. And this complexity and simplicity at the same time somehow have to proceed and co-exist. Nothing disappears when the truth of being is revealed and nothing gets added either. Life continues with all its vicissitudes just as before—in the space of clear knowing. It took me years of quietly digesting, processing and embodying the experience before I could start to write about it. The experience set a lot in motion in order for life to accommodate the *Knowing*. This will be described in the second book of the *Complete Humanity* series.

"Making simple things complex
is not an intelligence.
Making very complex things simple
is an intelligence"

Sadguru

PART 2.

Practical
Guidance Towards
Enlightenment:

Map and Directions

CHAPTER 4.

Clearing some Doubts, Opening the View

4.1 WHAT IS ENLIGHTENMENT?

This entire part of the book is about how to dip into enlightenment. I know this is a bold statement and I wouldn't make it if I wasn't sure that it is possible. I also know how even the most sincere, long-term, spiritual search only increases the doubt that enlightenment can be possible, but I want to overturn your doubts entirely by the time you finish reading this section.

Let's first define enlightenment. *Enlightenment is the realization of one's true nature.* At the moment of enlightenment, what we think we are is gone and who we truly are is revealed. One instant we think we are someone, and the next we are gone as that person and yet still here. What changed is the *knowing* of who we are. "It is only a tacit understanding," said Huang Po. That's all. Even a short dip into enlightenment wakes up the mind from the strong identification as the separate solid human we call ourselves, and reveals our true nature. The recognition is instantaneous. We then proceed in life being awake to our true nature, while living this human character which we carry at the same time.

I am using the word "enlightenment" without a capital E. I am not undervaluing this experience, but at the same time I do not want to mislead you with the false expectation that you will live in perpetual bliss after tasting your true nature. Reading a menu in a restaurant—or even *tasting* the food—will not give you the same experience as eating it. Similarly, there is more to live here as this human after the Recognition. (This is the subject of the next book in this series.)

Because I am a storyteller, my map and directions to awaken the mind are in stories and in guided meditations—clear instructions on how to focus attention to release the mind's habitual identifications. In storytelling, I am able to present very potent teachings in a most unassuming way, a way that is easier for the mind to consider in order for inquiry to peel away the self-identity it has been carrying unknowingly. You do not need to read or implement all the guidance; just choose what feels right or interesting to experiment with, and play with it in your life.

4.2 IS ENLIGHTENMENT POSSIBLE? IS IT POSSIBLE FOR YOU?

I know these questions well! I have read libraries full of books on spirituality and found myself doubting: "Is it possible?" And later: "Is it possible for me?"

Let me be straightforward here. Enlightenment may happen at any moment, and at the same time enlightenment can't happen to you. *You* can't get enlightened. It is not possible for you. For the *you* who is identified now with the person you are (the one who is seeking), it is not possible. *Enlightenment is possible, but not for the seeker.* "Liberation is never *for* the person, it is always *from* the person," said the famous teacher Nisargadatta. This sounds like a riddle and it *is* one for the thinking mind, but be assured that it will be solved at the moment of enlightenment. Trying to solve it with the thinking mind itself will only bring tension and frustration. We can't solve the problem with the wrong tool. We can't use the mind to let go of itself. We can't see the white screen in the movie theater while the movie is running. As soon as the movie ends, the screen itself is revealed to the eye.

Huang Po would say to seekers: "Rid yourself of conceptual thought in a flash." This was his bold and uncompromising teaching. I didn't know how to stop the thought that was already present. In all my years of meditation, I never was able to stop the thought on demand. The Tibetan master Tulku Urgyen Rinpoche said: "Even if you detonate and destroy all the buildings you can't do it with thought; it's going to be there anyway!" The more doable teaching by Huang Po then came to me: "Be still. Do nothing." It didn't mean only be still in a physical body and don't do any action, but rather: "Stop engaging in any thought movement. Stop even the subtle striving to stop."

4.3 IS ENLIGHTENMENT SUDDEN OR GRADUAL?

Once I attended a talk by a famous writer and all I remember from it is the title: *Twenty Years to Overnight Success*. How brilliantly this also describes the path of the spiritual seeker! Do we have a choice in *how* the enlightenment experience happens or *when* we are able to let go of the deep core belief of being a separate *me* that holds us in ignorance? There are many proponents of the idea of sudden enlightenment and Huang Po was one of them. But he also was wise enough to know that if someone was not able to wake up right in the moment, then they had no choice in the matter. He would send them off to meditate intensely for seven years.

When I talk in this book about going around and around on the Seeker's Train with all the different spiritual modalities and methods, I also acknowledge that the seeker has no choice but to be on that train until the mind is able let go of the core ignorance. And at the same time enlightenment can happen any moment, if you are ready! And the very fact that you are reading this book means that there is enough mind capacity to wake up.

4.4 DO YOU NEED A TEACHER?

If you have access to a teacher and you resonate with him, it's certainly a gift. But the teacher does not necessarily have to be a human being in the physical form, sitting in front of you. Anything can be a teacher if you let it: an insight that suddenly comes to you, your own family, a house pet, Nature, books, videos, recordings, your boss, your job, any relationship, any circumstance, anything.

We usually need someone to lead us through uncharted territory and this is why in the beginning of the spiritual path we often gravitate to someone who can show us the way: where to go and how. At the same time what works in the beginning might become an obstacle later on. If we still place authority outside ourselves, on a teacher or guru, we keep an illusion that there is a separation between where we are and where our teacher is. Helpful though the teacher may be, attachment to him might be the biggest obstacle on any path to awakening. A masterful teacher recognizes when the student needs to be sent away, and will trick the student if he is resisting the separation.

I had one traditional teacher, Doug Spitz, but the way I was taught was very nontraditional. When I met him, I didn't speak English well. The way Doug spoke and what he was telling me all produced a resonance in my being; I *knew* what he was saying. Something in me knew what he was talking about, bypassing the thinking. The thinking mind would check out because it would not recognize certain words and I had only one choice: tune in to my teacher's being and have an experience of resonance.

He told me the reason why Jesus had not one, but twelve major disciples. Each of them, corresponding to his natural abilities, would be able to take in only part of Jesus' teachings. One would take a teaching intellectually, another would take it in through feeling, or the body, or through knowing; the twelve of them as a whole could then take in the teachings of Jesus in their entirety.

Huang Po, who died in AD 850, is an example of a teacher I never met, but who spoke to me in my last retreat. His wisdom came to my mind whenever I needed guidance. After Huang Po led me into the enlightenment experience, I started to notice that I was now led and guided by Life itself. Everything around me, everyone, every situation and every circumstance had become my teacher. I no longer needed guidance from someone else; guidance was everywhere. Every detail in my life had become a silent teacher. I was simply learning to read the

Book of Life in which words are perceived objects and people, and sentences are circumstances and relationships. I have learned to read my own story, which is the visible representation of my mind state in the moment.

There is nothing outside of our own mind. Everything *outside* is a holographic representation of the mind state—isn't that the best teacher ever?! It is always there, always available; you need only learn how to understand the teacher's language.

Trust that in any moment of your journey, the teacher is always present. If you can't find him/her/it, make an invocation in yourself, a silent prayer to open you to a teaching in any shape or form that will be just right for you in that moment. Ask in your invocation for guidance to come. Then get very quiet, attentive, and be ready to receive.

4.5 DO YOU NEED TO BELONG TO A TRADITIONAL PATH?

Please don't think that in order to receive teachings you must have a formal affiliation with some sort of organization or be a member of a spiritual community. At times, such an affiliation can serve as an escape from realization: we just get too comfortable in the familiar setting. It's no wonder we start to call everyone there *family*. It is a very comforting feeling to be surrounded by people who are trying to go in the same direction. It can, though, create a situation in which we all forget what we are really seeking. As humans, we like the feeling of belonging. It creates a nurturing bond, but it can also prevent us from exploring outside the established framework.

I recall Adyashanti talking about what pushed him to look outside of Zen after 15 years of complete devotion to that path. There was a conversation between some people in a dining hall. They were talking about how, after a decade or more of serious meditation, they were still not sure if they would ever reach enlightenment, but they were okay with it. These Zen practitioners were settled into their familiar practice routine, their beloved community, and were almost satisfied. The bittersweet flavor of their conversation struck Adyashanti to the core; he was not about to settle for anything less than enlightenment. So he started to look for truth in alternative ways. He would go to a cafe after work and write. He would pose a question to himself and start answering it, peeling layer by layer, getting more and more honest, until he would reach the core. It was this willingness to step outside of traditional practices which later led him to the enlightenment experience.

Doug Spitz recognized from the beginning that I was not cut out for the official gatherings that were held every week in Manhattan in an old brownstone, which was the home of the Gurdjieff Foundation. He brought me several times to different meetings there, mostly to ask me at the end how it was for me. I wasn't thrilled with the whole thing: sitting on hard chairs in a circle in a hot, tiny room, waiting for everyone to speak, my anxiety building up to the point where I was unable to speak when my turn came. I could not express myself verbally. I would lose access to English words. He also noticed it was hard for me to follow rules, so he figured out that the best way for me to hear and take in the teachings was to experience them in a place where I could relax. He followed this observation, this intuition, by inviting me to places where I could eat, relax and then listen with my full attention.

Over the years we went to many different restaurants in Midtown Manhattan, where I received the teachings. "Wow," you might wonder, "what kind of Dharma is that?!" Someone actually said that to me when I later shared my story in a spiritual gathering, and I realized that I should probably keep the restaurants out of my "spiritual story." I can tell you from my experience that it was exactly what I needed at the time. Anything else and I would have quit by the third try, but I couldn't resist a good lunch where I was both told a story and well fed! I would relax and let the teachings penetrate me without really understanding them fully. It was as if the teachings fused with me in some way. Where they went, I didn't know; I definitely couldn't repeat them. Sometime later, though, I began to make sense of what Doug was saying and I started to have some deep existential feelings and altered mind state experiences. I was expanding in my being.

CHAPTER 5.

How to Start, Right Where You Are

5.1 QUESTION EVERYTHING

Come back to your natural curiosity. If you are interested in self-realization, you will question all that you think you know. As children, we ask questions. As adults, we ask less and less. This is because we accept all the answers we've been given as truth and we never ask again.

I was a very annoying child for my mother. I remember pointing to things and asking the same question many times: "What is this? What is *this*?" It was as if I refused to accept the idea that *one word* could represent the whole mystery that I was experiencing. My mother tried her best to answer me calmly. Then she would raise her voice a little and finally she would snap at me: "I told you 100 times already, it's *rain!*" "Rain," I would repeat, and forever after, the label *rain* was installed in my mind for the event I had experienced as water droplets falling from the sky onto my face while I felt such joy and amazement, trying to catch them with my tongue. And so it is that for every event in life there are words and labels. Eventually all the world becomes solid, defined objects and instead of experiencing the immediacy of life we live in a world of *descriptions* of what life is, a world of labels.

I am still fascinated by the way language compartmentalizes reality, how the vastness of life gets reduced to words which are then presented as the reality. A map that represents some terrain is not the terrain itself. We know this well and we never confuse the one with the other, but when it comes to *words*, we take them to be the description of *reality* itself.

As soon as we are told what something *is*, we

stop questioning and our mind forms a static view. With a static view, we do not question anything and we therefore meet the world in an unconscious way. We accept what we are told and we lose curiosity, creativity, interest, questioning, pondering. We walk through a landscape and instead of enjoying the surroundings with all their beauty and mystery, we peer at the map, reading: "this is the road," "this is a forest," "this is a pond," "this is the sky," "this is a tree." No wonder we are not inspired anymore: we are lost among all these labels and the perceived predictability.

5.2 FOLLOW YOUR NATURAL INTEREST

If you just follow your interest, whatever the activity is, you will be engaged in it wholeheartedly—with all your might—instead of trying to do something because your thinking tells you that you should. *Attention naturally flows to where one's interest is.* If you want a relationship, fall in love with a man or a woman; if you want to wake up, fall in love with the truth. Attention, focused in one direction, will point the way home into the arms of the beloved. This is the magic of trusting your natural interest to guide you. As the 13th-Century Persian poet Rumi said, "Your heart knows the way, run in that direction."

Once I was working with someone in a guided inquiry. We lived in a retreat center, and we were sitting outside the dining area. While I was trying to focus his attention on our work, I noticed his eyes were following every girl passing by—and there were a lot of pretty girls in this retreat center! At first, I allowed this to just be, noticing if his attention would naturally return back to work. But by the fifth or sixth girl, I knew what was most important for this man at this time. He had been a spiritual seeker for a long time and had developed a very strong belief that seeking the truth was most important for him. However, if he were to be very honest with himself, he would notice where his attention naturally went. And if he were to follow his natural interest, he would go in the direction of exploring a relationship at this time of his life.

Following your interest seems like a distraction on the seeker's path. We try to avoid engaging with it, but the attention doesn't give a damn what we think; it just flows with the interest. To realize our true nature, to wake up to who we are, requires full, undivided attention: each moment, each day, for any duration of time. This realization is not satisfied with 80% attention on inner inquiry and 20% on your responsibilities and curiosity in other areas, not even 90/10. What it requires is 100% attention: full focus. If you find yourself interested in anything else besides inquiry, if you notice you are still thinking about some other things you want to do, just go do them. Meet friends, travel, party, build your business, make babies: do whatever pulls you most at this time. There will be a time when you have tried it all and at that very moment, nothing will be more important for you than realizing your true nature. When all of your attention, 100% of it, becomes transfixed on this inquiry only, you enter into a very potent inner environment where enlightenment is possible.

If we don't follow our natural interest honestly, we engage in life activities in a way that doesn't give proper attention to any of them and we find ourselves living unsatisfied, mediocre lives.

5.3 DON'T ASK FOR PERMISSION

We are so conditioned to ask for permission! I know this firsthand. I was born and raised in the socialist USSR, where everything was structured to keep people in line. There was a rule for everything and you had to ask for permission to do anything. But I don't ask for permission anymore; I stopped asking long ago.

I am one of the co-founders of Liberation Unleashed, a network of volunteer guides to the realization of the selfless nature of being. In collaboration, we developed a method to point the mind to selflessness without any preliminary spiritual practice. Everyone involved brought their own piece of the puzzle to put together a potent method of self-inquiry we called *Direct Pointing*. When we were bringing forth Liberation Unleashed, some established spiritual teachers were against this method. If we had asked for permission, we would still be going around in circles trying to make everyone feel heard and important.

Please understand that there are no real authorities, only perceived ones. The self-identity, full of limiting beliefs, projects its perception of authorities, rules, regulations and structures. If you decide to step outside the circle, box, or organization, you do not need permission. Just take the first step out and feel the freedom. Anything that has come forth into existence—through anyone—has a right to exist. This is why nothing stopped us from creating Liberation Unleashed. We asked for no previous experience in any spiritual modality and no list of spiritual achievements from the inquirers.

We asked only for their 100% attention in the no-self inquiry dialogue. Some established teachers would oppose "revealing" the inner teachings of selflessness without years of preliminary practice. At times, I too had concerns; I had been a practitioner of the Buddhist Vipassana meditation method for many years and knew the value of 10,000 hours of meditation in gradually developing insight, ethics, deep mindfulness and concentration. But the power of intention to wake people up from self-identification was so strong that Liberation Unleashed was born. It didn't need permission from the thinking mind—not mine or anyone else's.

5.4 STEP OUT OF THE WELL-TRAVELED PATH

For centuries, people would tend to notice exactly what brought them to self-realization. They would try to document it, to somehow structure the path for others and pass it on. I have documented my experience too, just to give you a taste of the possibility. Unfortunately, one person's path is not another's. In fact, if you feel like you are walking a path that was clearly laid out by someone else, if you see more than one set of footprints right behind you, get off! Leave that path and venture into unknown territory. Only then will you have a chance. At the end of a path walked by someone else, there may, at most, be a book about her own experience, a song, a poem, or a silent look into your eyes.

I was very devoted to the Vipassana meditation path and yet at one point I had to leave the path traveled by millions. In the end, I cut my own path and if you try to follow me you will only arrive at frustration. Maybe then, when you are pissed off at me because my path doesn't work for you, you will stop blindly following—me or anyone else.

Having said this, there *are* signs, little lanterns on the path that will shine just enough to show you your first step off the traveled path. For me, it was the "Who Am I?" question. I had read a book of Ramana Maharshi's in which he explained the "Who am I?" method, but honestly, I didn't get it. I knew there was a path this man walked and that he was trying to give his map to others, but most of us can't read his map properly. Some, like me, just throw the map out into the first garbage bin we see, and go back to our routine so we at least understand logically what we are doing. Others will take the map and read everything written on the map, but won't even take the first step forward. Still others take the map and put it on their altar as a picture of the man who wrote the map, and they bow to it, pray to it, light candles by it. I am not making fun of anyone here; everyone just does what they think they should do. This is very crucial to understand: we walk the best we can, innocently, based on our conditioned thinking.

Ramana's "Who am I?" lantern is still there and there is no need to carry his book with you, to read it many times or to go to his ashram in India (although I did, just to see that his lantern is not limited to the cave he was in when he woke up with this very question alive in him). Once you have come across the "Who am I?" lantern and have seen the light, it's in you, and when the time and conditions are right, it will suddenly illuminate the limiting darkness of the conceptual mind. And it will be in a way that is unique for you.

5.5 LET GO OF CALCULATING THE FASTEST WAY

In hindsight, I know now that every detail was important for the experience of self-realization which I've described. Even if I had known all this in advance and tried to align everything perfectly, there would still have been no guarantee of it. I've come to understand that in the end, it's pure Grace that responds to the human yearning to know oneself, and the outcome can't be calculated in advance. There are just too many variables—an infinite number of variables—and the human mind can't even know exactly what it was in that matrix of variables that culminated in the enlightenment experience.

Some common denominators have been noticed and are described in various teachings. Frameworks have been built to facilitate the perfect conditions for the mind to awaken. But still, in practice there is a point when all these efforts fail. One teacher might say that effort is essential, while another might say that it is essential that there be no effort. And this is usually just confusing, because the understanding will be led by thinking: to make an effort, or to try not to make any effort. And then one strives to apply effort while another strives to let go of effort, but the revelation of truth happens when there is no thinking and no thinker! Then the truth that might have been spoken before (but was not actually heard) suddenly speaks again: "Who Am I?" The lantern left on the path by a previous traveler still shines in Consciousness and it may light up just a little patch for you to step on. Trust that it is enough for you to know just this very step, and the moment after it will give you the next one.

CHAPTER 6.

What Tools are Good to Have?

6.1 MAKE FRIENDS WITH SILENCE

Silence is not overrated! Silence is the catalyst. True, deep silence may open the doors to completely different perceptions. Why am I saying *true*? We may not talk with anyone all day, but we typically talk to *ourselves* constantly and don't even notice it! We may even have the impression that we have spent all day in silence, especially if we are in a retreat. Surely, we have been in silence—the retreat even says so in its description: "*Silent* retreat"! Oh, I have been in such retreats too many times not to know the truth of this! The mind gets even louder after a day of silence and by the second day you want to run away from your own head! But if you continue to abstain from talking, you will eventually come to a relatively calm mind. Every question presented to your mind at this point will have exponentially more power. You will get an answer. Keep silence, keep asking.

Once I was in a silent retreat at the Omega Institute in Rhinebeck, New York (Page 37), and most of the day we were sitting in meditation. After the mind settled, I introduced it to a series of questions that were suggested before the meditation. "Where is the leg?" I asked inwardly and I found myself looking at the leg. "Where is the hand?" I asked and found myself looking at the hand. As the question was asked, the attention went there. "Where is I?" I asked. Suddenly, the I who was asking the questions was gone. The attention pointed me back to myself and now I was Awareness. My body was sitting on the cushion, looking around, and I was everything that sees. I spent almost an entire week in an amazing mind state of *being Awareness*, just sitting in that retreat in silence. Although it was not the end of the search for me, this was an important experience of breaking the identification with *me* as the *physical body and thinking mind.*

Silence: yes, yes, and yes to it! Do this experiment at home. Fill a mason jar with water. Then put a handful of sand in it and shake it. Put it on a table and observe how opaque the water is with all the sand floating around. Keep looking at it, seeing the water as the mind and the sand as thoughts. If you leave the jar still, you will see at some point how the sand starts to settle and, in time, the water becomes clear again. Try to have periods in your life where you can be like the motionless mason jar. Let thoughts naturally settle, uncovering the clear nature of the mind. Only then go ahead and ask your favorite potent question, the one that is already there and trying to voice itself. For me it was "Who am I?" and all the variations of this question. You might have your own inquiry, depending on what is already present in you as a question.

6.2 OWN YOUR OWN BODY

If you have a secret wish to resolve this enlightenment thing in your head, I will tell you right now that this is as attainable as to think into existence an elephant in your living room. A friend once told me that 20 years of *satsangs* only gave him serious headaches while trying to "understand"! He turned to somatic practices to start to feel his own body. I know this sounds contradictory, since so many teachings point out that there is no body, and the experience of enlightenment brings one to realize that the physical world—including your own body— is all mind creation. But in order to come to this realization, one must own one's own body first, then deconstruct it to directly experience that it doesn't exist. Otherwise, the awakening will be incomplete.

The energies that descend into the body during these types of mind expansions are humongous, and the body won't be able to process them properly, presenting serious physical problems.

If you feel like all of your life is going in your own head, then this message is for you. What do I mean by *owning your own body*? Isn't it obvious, you may ask, that everyone has one? What I mean is to FEEL the body, feel the sensations of the body, feel its emotions, feel it as a living organism, not just as the sum of legs, trunk, hands and neck on which the head sits.

It is very common in the West for spiritual seekers to do all of their work in the head. I will tell you what some of the teachers I have encountered would do for this kind of aspirant when he would come and ask to be guided to enlightenment.

G.I. Gurdjieff was famous for his meetings in New York City in the early 20th Century, where he would prepare a feast consisting of some lamb stew and Armaniac—the special Georgian liquor. He served dinner before any teachings or discussions, and made everyone eat and drink a couple of shots, regardless of whether they were vegetarians or nondrinkers—or both. Though it can be seen as violent (and I am not a proponent of this method), it was Gurdjieff's way of bringing people into their bodies, away from their habitual thinking. Only when everyone shifted from the head into the body would he offer the teachings. So it's clear that his teaching started with a lamb stew!

Reggie Ray, a student of Chogyam Trungpa Rinpoche, the Tibetan Buddhist teacher, developed another method to bring people's attention to the body they own. He would offer retreats where people would be encouraged to lie down, put their feet on the floor, knees together and in this position meditate on the sensations of the body, going from head to toes. When they had felt the body fully, the participants would then sit up on the cushion to continue their meditation. My ex-husband, who was very analytical and cerebral, attended Reggie Ray's first year-long training. Between this training and my constantly pointing him to feel his feet (which later on we laughed about!), he started to feel sensations in his body that he had not been aware of for almost 50 years!

Mr. Goenka's method of Vipassana meditation is fully focused on the sensations of the body and this is very helpful for many at some point in their search. You can simply sign up for one of the free courses they hold continuously during the year in many centers worldwide. Dancing, yoga and any movement are helpful to begin feeling your body again. No-hurry lovemaking with someone special touching your body is an excellent way to start to feel sensations. Gentle, nurturing massage—or indeed any modality that has a gentle touch to the body—can be very helpful.

I will tell you how I first started to feel my body. I must say that prior to this experience, I had no idea that I wasn't feeling my body. I wasn't even thinking about it. I assumed that this was how it was supposed to be: here was my body, I saw it, I knew it, and I didn't need to think anything more about it.

At the time, in the year 2000, I was very much into yoga. I loved it and I did yoga every day, eventually becoming a certified yoga instructor. As part of my studies, I attended a workshop on Phoenix Rising Yoga Therapy. In this modality, a practitioner facilitates yoga postures for a client, holding the posture and asking simple questions like "What do you feel right now?"

The experience I want to share occurred in a practice session in which I was *the client* and another workshop participant was *the practitioner*.

The practitioner spread my arms to the sides and bent and moved one of my legs over my body, gently turning me in a side stretch. "What do you feel now?" she asked me. At this point, I experienced something that I had never experienced before or—as I concluded later—something I had forgotten, my body had forgotten. Through the years of hardships and living in survival mode after immigration, I had somehow contracted myself into the thinking head. While I was lying there, held by my exercise facilitator, I experienced a rush of sensations through my whole body and I suddenly started to feel my legs and body parts in a very distinct way. As sensations rushed through my limbs, the feeling overwhelmed me and tears poured out of me like a sudden rain. As the floodgates opened in me, a stream of sensations and feelings that had been forgotten and suppressed somewhere in the depths of the psyche rushed into awareness. After the exercise, I went outside and walked the streets of Manhattan, wandering aimlessly, fascinated by the simple act of walking and feeling the sensations in my body, in every part, every little square inch. I was alive again!

6.3 BEFRIEND AN AWAKE "ORDINARY SCHMUCK"

Maybe you have heard the word *sangha*, which is often translated as *community* but it is really more a commune of students studying with someone who had an enlightenment experience and can guide others to realize their true nature. These beings are examples of the possibility of enlightenment and it is very important to really know that it is possible. If they don't look like a teacher, if they look like your next-door neighbor, or if they are going through some difficulties in life and maybe at times don't look at all like someone who *knows*, even better! As the Dzogchen teacher Allan Wallace once said, there is value in a teacher being "an ordinary schmuck." It can make you really believe that enlightenment is not some unachievable goal that is bestowed only on a few in a century; rather it is possible at every moment for anyone.

When my teacher Doug Spitz told me that he was aware *from breath to breath*, it opened up a possibility for me. Anyone who has tried meditation knows it is not easy to be present with everything without slipping into thinking or daydreaming, and in daily life it is even more difficult. But hearing Doug say it was possible to be aware all the time made it possible for me. If I had read a book about it, I would certainly be impressed but I would still doubt. Watching my teacher closely for many years confirmed the possibility for me. Several years later, I too became aware *from breath to breath*.

Being close to someone who is awakened will teach you that he is not an almighty wonder-being: someone who has lost all reactiveness, does not experience emotions, is in perfect health, has no physical or emotional pain, and smiles all the time. Different stimuli will still evoke emotions, but this becomes a very spontaneous event and passes quickly—like a child who falls down, cries out in sudden pain and then quickly forgets about the pain and looks in wonder at a fascinating little rock on the ground!

Our minds have a lot of ideas of what an awakened human being looks like. But what if your teacher is... not a vegetarian? ...doesn't sit in a pretzel pose in meditation all day? ...doesn't greet everyone in the local grocery store by saying, "Namaste"? What if she ...is married and affectionate with her mate? ... drinks wine and talks politics at dinner with friends? ...works in a corporation or trades stocks at night? I am not saying that what I mention here is correct for everyone, but what is correct for an awake, conscious being is purely individual, spontaneous, comes from a natural interest, and involves a certain equilibrium of the mind with an efficient use of energy and biological resources. Like a child who plays spontaneously, the awakened one is in a similar state of play with life's demands and events. There are no *spiritual* and *unspiritual* activities; there is simply a spontaneity and playfulness with any activity.

6.4 USE EVERY SITUATION FOR PRACTICE

Stop trying to fix your life. One day you may find that you were trying to rearrange the furniture in your house in order to feel better, only to find later on that the whole house needed demolition because it was built on the wrong foundation.

Work with what you've got. If you live with a partner who is difficult to be around, instead of trying to fix them, inquire deeper into your own feelings and thoughts. Study your own reactions until you are clear within yourself how exactly this mechanism of annoyance works. People would come to G.I. Gurdjieff to complain about someone who was living with them at the institute Gurdjieff had created for practice. If many people complained about the same person, Gurdjieff would make sure that person was offered all kinds of incentives to stay at the institute to continue to irritate people so they wouldn't have any choice but to inquire about what was driving their reaction. Having said that, in some cases you will find that completely stepping out from involvement may be the best choice in a situation. Trying to fix the other person, or trying to adjust to the situation by being inauthentic yourself are surely the least beneficial options.

How do you deal with difficult people? Here's where I can finally tell you why waking up is so important! Tolerance toward difficult people or situations can be developed, but it is almost as if one is holding a spiral coil under tension all the time; it takes a lot of energy to be tolerant. When the mind is awake, there is a deep understanding that everyone is God, but they may not know it yet. What is talking the loudest in some people is the pain of perceived separation, and the ignorance of the conditioned mind that is trying to resolve this pain through any means it can. There is no way to really understand and to follow the Bible's advice: "If anyone slaps you on the right cheek, turn to him the other also", without understanding the fundamental truth that *there are no others*. To understand this is to wake up to this truth in your own being.

6.5 RETURN TO A CHILDLIKE ATTITUDE

Earlier I described how I wanted to wake people up in a meditation hall: "It's all an illusion! Go do something better with your lives!" But almost immediately, I understood that I don't know what is best for anyone other than myself. You know what's right for you because you know where your attention falls most often; you know what draws your attention again and again like a magnet. So, whether it is sitting for two hours in meditation or traveling, studying or anything else—you know it better than me.

My message here is: "Don't forget to smile. Please don't go into meditation as you would go to war to conquer an enemy." It was just like that at some point for me: very serious! It's the same with anything in life. The story—that most of us hold so dearly as though it were our life—*is* a story and can be lightened up at any moment by stopping and smiling, being almost mischievous: "This is difficult, but it's interesting, let's see what happens!" A smile can turn the whole scene around. Try to smile at life itself and invite yourself and others to play, building castles in a sandbox instead of installing steel bars and pouring concrete.

When I was a little girl, I used to make dolls out of hollyhock flowers. Every doll would die at the end of the day, her flower dress wilted. Even though I would create a whole story for my doll, the story would be over by the end of the day. The next day would bring a different doll and a different story. For some time, I forgot how to play, especially when I got married, emigrated to a different country, and had a child. Life was tough and I was very serious. Since then, I have lived in many different circumstances, in a couple of marriages, in different towns. Just like with my hollyhock dolls, there have been different stories that would end and new ones that would start afterwards. I grow hollyhocks now in my backyard and they remind me of the impermanence of life's stories. They inspire an attitude of playfulness that is always available.

CHAPTER 7.

What to Avoid

7.1 AVOID THE TRAP OF FASCINATION

How many times have we heard someone return from a retreat or a workshop saying that this was the most profound experience of their life and that now they *really* know? I've been a friend of many who were involved in different spiritual circles and I witnessed *The Return* many times. My own experience with different mind states throughout my practice only deepened my understanding of impermanence.

Impermanence is a Buddhist term, *anicca* in the ancient Sanskrit language. It defines the material world as ever-changing. We think we know what impermanence is until we go to the next retreat or have the next experience, the next journey. Then we return all blissed out and absolutely sure that this is it and this is how we will be from now on.

I don't want to be a buzz killer, so I often feel like I don't know what to say when I am told the next story of *this is it*. Actually, I do know what I want to say, but I also know it will not work at that moment. I know that experiences of this sort are a grand show of the human mind and certainly they transform old brain patterns to some degree, but with time the experience fades. Once, in a noisy airport, as we were coming back from a retreat together, Doug Spitz said with a smirk, "Isn't it life coming on us like a ton of bricks?" He was pointing me to the change in a mind state, and to the fact that this is inevitable.

I don't want to underestimate the value of such experiences; they definitely create an opening in the mind, a new understanding. But I also don't want to overemphasize it and add even more to the fascination. Fascination is a mind state in itself and it too is impermanent. Enlightenment is a deep knowing of the impermanence of apparent world phenomena and a realization of the nature of the mind as boundless and beyond transitory experiences. No wonder human life is a duality that needs not to be rejected, but realized intimately. At the enlightenment moment, the mind knows its true nature and in the next moment, the mind is contracted to its usual human busyness. We perceive some experiences to be mystical, superhuman or transcendent, but they too come to an end and we find ourselves back into very human, so-called mundane states.

If we really study impermanence by way of meditation, contemplation, or even life-long observation, we will see that it is something that permeates every experience, mundane or transcendent. The very base of any experience is impermanence. To learn that, to notice it and wonder at the impermanence itself, is more reliable and gratifying than the fascination with the transcendent mind states themselves. Sooner or later they change, leaving us in the restless state of wanting and longing for something more than what is present at this very moment—a state that is in itself the source of human suffering.

7.2 BEWARE OF SPIRITUAL PRIDE

I had been seeking intensely for years prior to waking up and I sometimes bemoaned how long it seemed to take me to let go of all wrong expectations, ideas and beliefs. The path—with all its twists and turns—seems so clear to me now: why I turned this way, why I went in that direction. Every turn and every back road was absolutely necessary to let go of those beliefs.

If someone took 20 years to walk the path, then it was absolutely necessary for them to take 20 years. If someone else walked the path in no time at all, that was just right for them. No pride should be attached to the number of years spent walking on the path. What is there to be proud of? Years of crawling on back roads in the mud of the mind's constructed bullshit?!

Buddhists believe that one of the 10 *fetters* (translated as the chains that keep us bound to this plane of existence and force us to be reborn) is conceit or spiritual pride. I was guilty of this myself; therefore, I can warn you about this trap and, if you happened to fall into it already, try to look at it with a new perspective.

I have much respect for the spiritual path and for anyone who walks on it for a long time, for anyone who grinds every obstacle to dust before proceeding further. I have just the same respect for anyone who walks skipping and whistling joyfully with a flower in her hair, gently caressed by the wind. Everyone will live their share of life in their own unique way and every life has my deepest respect.

The years I spent serving my time on the

path didn't make me any better. Perhaps they imprinted in me more pride that I had to deal with later. I noticed how I perceived myself as a "hardcore" meditator, as someone who had sat for the traditionally recommended ten thousand hours of meditation. What difference does that make now, when I know that from seeking to enlightenment can take only one breath? I can only laugh at myself for being so stubborn in my ways, and laugh at the whole notion of the path.

7.3 DITCH EXPECTATIONS

This is a big one. We all read books about *perfectly enlightened* men and women and we are sure we know how enlightened ones should look and behave. We project our expectations onto our teachers, idealizing them. Please save yourself many years of meditation towards enlightenment. Assume that you don't actually know how it is until you yourself have the experience of realization.

The biggest obstacle on the way to realization is having expectations—of any kind. If you expect that the path is long and it is a step-by-step progression for several lifetimes then you won't even notice that the very truth you are looking for is already here. It is possible to see it at any moment, but you keep walking step by step because this is how you think it should be. Or, if you are someone who assumes that enlightenment equals sainthood, you will have doubts that it is possible for you. "Maybe it is possible for this teacher," you think, since you idealized them in the first place, "but for me, with all my emotions, reactions, and imperfections, it is surely impossible." Please accept my invitation to become close to someone who you suspect is *enlightened* or *awake*, and notice the many things about them that will help you to let go of the idea that you have to be perfect in every way to know the truth. Everyone falls into this trap of expecting from enlightenment some extraordinary abilities, non-reactiveness, or *no thinking*. These expectations delay our liberation.

A friend of mine was once looking for a specific healer, a shaman woman in Mexico. My friend looked for this healer everywhere, asking everyone at a certain town market for several months if they knew her. At last, she came across someone who said that she would bring her to the healer's home. With much excitement and some trepidation, my friend followed this woman from the market for a long time until they reached a little hut in the forest. There was no one there and my friend asked the woman where the shaman was. The woman said she would go get her and disappeared into the hut. After some time, when my friend had started to worry that something was not right, the same woman came out of the house. And yet she was not the same. Her eyes, her posture, her being were completely transformed. She was the shaman, the healer my friend was looking for. And how many times, looking for a *shaman*, she had passed that unassuming woman at the market without a second glance!

7.4 LET GO OF ATTACHMENT TO EXTERNAL METHODS

Please don't be fooled by your wishful thinking that something from outside can free you. Rely on your own inquiry, on your ability to focus attention and on your own discernment. These are the essential elements in the search for truth; you can develop them and they will be with you regardless of where you are. All the electronic devices and programs that help to induce alpha brainwaves, all the plants and substances that alter mind states won't help you if you are somewhere without access to them or if you do not have the money to pay for them. Please rely instead on your own inquiry.

Ayahuasca is one of the plant medicines that helped my ex-husband, a mental health professional, at the beginning of his spiritual journey. He first took the hallucinogenic brew in 1999 and it freed him from the concrete belief that the world is rock solid. For a medical doctor rooted in science, this was a somewhat shocking experience. He saw that objects are not solid; instead they appeared to him more as an energy movement. Objects appeared and disappeared as he watched their movement right in front of him with his eyes wide open. This was truly a revelation, a beginning of his inquiry into what the mind really is—not what he learned about it in medical school, not from all his knowledge of psychiatry, but from direct experience. The experience opened him to a new understanding of the world we see as only one variation of the perception. This was a big opening—don't get me wrong. I knew how significant this was for him! But don't get stuck in the *journeying*, year after year. I met many who did. They formed an attachment to the altered mind states and mistook them for the clarity that arises from *real knowing*.

7.5 STOP FEARING THE FEAR

As soon as you make a step towards knowing who you are, even a tiny step, fear will be right there. You may have noticed it before—or you may notice it as soon as we start to dip into the next section.

Here it is useful to know what fear is. Fear is a feeling. Its job has a simple description: protection. Have you noticed how it shows up every time we are about to go into the unknown? Fear is very consistent. We can look at fear as an absolutely reliable friend. Isn't it comforting to know that any time there is a danger we won't be left without a warning from fear to prepare for the danger? This is crucial to understand. Fear is not our enemy;

it's a friend and we might treat it as such, with friendliness.

On the other hand, fear—as our friend—is a bit misled in this modern age. Fear was born in ancient times when early humans needed to survive all kinds of threats associated with living in the wild—from carnivorous animals, for example. In our age, the probability of meeting a tiger on the way to work is almost zero. Our friend fear doesn't really know that. It operates in an almost binary fashion, on or off:

> 0 - familiar = no threat = fear rests.
> 1 - unknown = threat = fear warns

Leaving an old job, relationship, environment, state of mind or belief, and venturing into new, unfamiliar territory, will wake fear up to fulfill its routine responsibilities. Fear takes its responsibilities very seriously; you can be assured that this friend will never leave you alone trekking through the dark forest without notifying you of even the slightest crack of a branch under a wild animal's foot.

As any friend does, fear requires open and honest communication. If you are about to do something new and you feel that you don't need fear's suggestions at this moment, you can handle the situation just like you would do with a friend. Start talking to fear as soon as it joins your company. Say "hi," for example. At least you will acknowledge to yourself that you are not alone. Treat fear as a friend, and instead of shutting the door in its face, invite it in for cookies and tea—and some honest conversation. You might start like this: "Hi, my friend! I know you came to warn me of a danger. You have been a very reliable friend to me for all these years and I appreciate you. Thank you very much for your work. Right now, there is no real danger around me, no wild animals, and I am not standing on the edge of the roof on my toes. I am in my room and all is well. I just want to inquire into something new, but there is no actual threat to my organism. So you may stay here, have some tea, relax. I will be doing some inquiries here and I promise I will not jump from the building; I will just get very attentive, open, and ask myself some questions. That's all. There is no need for you to protect me. You can just rest."

After you've had a friendly chat with fear, you can proceed with your inquiry without fear grabbing onto you like a crawling baby who clings to mommy for safety and acknowledgment. Now you can do your work.

CHAPTER 8.

How to Dip into Enlightenment, Now!

8.1 NOTICE THE SEEKER'S IDENTITY

We assume that spiritual seeking has a goal of *finding*, but let me tell you: I met so many who created an identity around it. I was one of them at one point too, *a serious spiritual seeker*! If you invite such a serious spiritual seeker to look into the heart of the matter and end the search, they will resist it in every way possible: whether in a subtle way with a smile as they drift away from you, or more openly with debates and clever arguments. They will protect their seeking. For many of us this is how we live life. Seeking gives us something to constantly be engaged with—an identity, an importance in our own eyes.

As long as there is the concrete identity, *I*

am a spiritual seeker, there will always be seeking. An identity assumes a someone who does a certain action. What action is the seeker doing? Seeking! No wonder you may hear from a teacher that "the seeking stops when the seeker disappears."

What if we look from the other side? Consider the notion that seeking does not really belong to you. If you have been seeking for some time already, you know exactly what I mean. *You* did not start the search; it just started one day and it will not stop when you decide it's enough. There is no control over seeking. Ask yourself this question: is there one who is seeking or is seeking just what is happening?

8.2 UNCOVER THE ILLUSION OF CHOICE

When you go to the supermarket to buy some food, notice how you choose, how the choices happen. You come to the bread section and choose whole-wheat bread, or gluten-free bread, or a French baguette, or organic ciabatta bread, or a loaf of Wonder bread. Before you grab the bread without a second thought, I invite you to investigate everything that happens *right before*. Stop for a second and look inside. You will notice that every choice has thoughts, beliefs and feelings associated with it. Beliefs are thoughts that we've thought so many times that we assume they are the truth for us. So, before we grab the bread, we already have a belief about what kind of bread is best for us. This belief was established via many sources: what our parents told us, what a doctor told us, or the media, or our friends. The sources that create a belief are endless, but ultimately what is important is that a belief is formed and then not questioned until a new source might point us to tweak the belief a little.

In the supermarket, the choice is made by a belief. Just as an experiment, take a Wonder bread loaf instead of the organic ciabatta that you like and stay there with it, noticing the thoughts and feelings that arise from not following the usual choice that is based on your belief. I am not asking you to buy Wonder bread in the end; I am only asking you to investigate what's behind the choices that we think are ours and how they come about.

Investigation of this sort takes time. It is an active pondering on all the events of your life—how you actually made that particular choice, married that particular partner, went into a certain profession. When you ask yourself the question, "How did I choose this?" you will get an immediate logical and obvious answer from the mind: "I studied to become a doctor because I loved the idea of being a professional and helping people." Please do not stop there. Question where that idea came from and you will start to see the signs of the mind leaning in a particular direction which has nothing to do with the choice itself. The direction was already there; at a certain moment, it manifested in the movement of sending an application to a medical school. See that you are not a decision maker, not a chooser, not a doer. The movement of choice happens in the unconscious mind long before—and then it becomes conscious, which creates the illusion of choice and doing.

You might like to look into some very interesting research by brain scientists which clearly shows that the *choice* of which button to press on a computer happens around seven seconds after the choice has actually been made in the brain of the participants. The thought "I will choose this option," which creates the illusion that the choice is *theirs*, happens after certain areas of the brain light up on a screen right before their eyes, indicating that the choice has already been made.

8.3 NOTICE THAT YOU ARE NOT THE MANAGER OF THE EXPERIENCE

Inhale. Exhale. Inhale. Exhale. Inhale. Exhale. Inhale. Exhale. Inhale. Exhale. Inhale. Exhale. Inhale. Exhale. Inhale... Notice that no one is doing it. The organism is carrying out its own program...

This thought. That thought. This thought. That thought. This thought. That thought. This thought. That thought... Notice that no one is doing it. The organism is carrying out its own program...

Warmth. Cold. Itching. Expansion. Contraction. Pain. Tension. Lightness. Warmth. Cold. Itching. Expansion. Contraction. Pain. Tension.

Lightness. Warmth... Notice that no one is doing it. The organism is carrying out its own program...

Sadness. Boredom. Anger. Guilt. Shame. Contentment. Peace. Joy. Irritation. Anxiety. Sadness. Boredom. Anger. Guilt. Shame. Contentment. Peace. Joy. Irritation. Anxiety. Sadness... Notice that no one is doing it. The organism is carrying out its own program...

8.4 REST IN OPEN AWARENESS LIKE A NEWBORN

Here is a simple but very potent exploration I created in the form of a guided meditation. There is a recording of this meditation. Just go to https://www.elenanezhinsky.com/buddha-on-a-bull if you want to use audio version.

Relax right where you are. Make yourself comfortable; you may even lie down or relax in a recliner. Close your eyes. Inhale and exhale deeply. Imagine yourself just after being born. You are a tiny baby in a crib and you have just been born today. You do not have a name yet. You can't understand human language yet; you are just lying there in the crib and breathing. The window to the room is open a bit and some fresh air from outside drifts into the room. You feel it on your skin. Since you were just born, you don't yet know your boundaries. You don't have knowledge of how humans name things; you are not yet thinking. You are just lying there and breathing. You are one with the experience. You are one with the gentle breeze, one with the room. You open your eyes and you are one with seeing. You do not see objects since you don't know them yet. You are just the *seeing* itself: the act of seeing without labeling the experience. You are one with the feeling, seeing, sensing. Maybe there are some hunger pains in the stomach: the mouth opens and cries come out. You are picked up and you feel the warmth of touch. You are one with that warm skin, one with the flow of milk coming into you. You are experiencing *being-ness* without any separation. You are seeing, hearing, touching, sensing, tasting, smelling—all six human senses without the thinking mind.

If you were following my guidance just now you are ready to open your eyes and—without getting right back to labeling objects—very slowly, like a baby, look around the room. Now with your eyes open, keep looking through the eyes of the you who's just been born. Because the thinking mind is not working in you yet, notice the difference in perception when you do not divide the world into objects by naming them *wall, ceiling, lamp*, etc. You are simply staring around, as a newborn baby, experiencing seeing. Be there in the undivided being-ness. Simply be. As you experience it in a new way—less concrete, less divided—notice how as a newborn baby you do not know the word "I" yet. You are one with the environment. There is no separation. As you continue to sit or lie, and look, you will notice that as the eyes fall onto an object, the mind will immediately offer a suggestion as to what it is: a *word-description*. Don't grasp onto that word; just keep imagining yourself as a newborn that does not know words yet. You will continue to experience in a new way, a way that you had forgotten. Also notice how the word-description comes, just a second after the experience itself. First there is the wordless experience and then the word comes. In this meditation, you can notice that the experience is what is real, what is really happening, and the name we give it is just a word, a label. In a different language, it will be a different word which can even have a slightly different meaning. So, let's just be with what *is* real: the experience itself.

8.5 LET'S UNINSTALL THE "I"

The enlightenment experience is a spontaneous event. As soon as the thought ceases and the focus is open, this is enlightenment. *You* are not enlightened. *You* are what you think yourself to be, always just out of reach for enlightenment to reveal itself. *You* and *enlightenment* cancel each other out like two mutually exclusive events. As soon as you get back to your usual conceptual mind state, the enlightenment is gone. As *enlightenment* is, *you* are not. Go figure.

At this point in our work together, your mind might already have given up figuring out and labeling, but if "I" appears in a thought, for example "I am cold" or "I am tired," try the following experiment:

Imagine you have an *Uninstall* button just like for any computer program. If we do not need a program, we uninstall it. Now we are going to uninstall the word "I" from the mind. Imagine that I am pressing an imaginary *Uninstall* button on you (you can actually press anywhere on your body as if there were a button there) and therefore uninstalling the word "I" from your mind. You, like a baby, do not have access to the word "I." If before there was the thought "I am cold," now instead it will be "It is cold." But what actually changed in your experience when we uninstalled the word "I"?

> Did you disappear?
>
> Are you still there?
>
> You are not the "I" thought.
>
> Thought can not read.
>
> Thought can not hear.
>
> What are you?

8.6 NOTICE THE BORDERLESS QUALITY OF THE EXPERIENCE

What are you without the word "I"?

What are you without the name?

As I pressed the *Uninstall* button that deleted the "I" thought, who are you now?

Ask: "Who am I?"

Remember, you do not have the thought "I" in your mind's library anymore. You can't pull it out and use it to answer this question. Ask yourself: "Where is *I*?"

Notice a much wider presence than just being in the body as the "I" thought.

Keep breathing and just be.

Notice the quality of presence that permeates everything.

In just experiencing without naming, there are no borders.

This experiencing reminds me of a symphony orchestra listened to with closed eyes: the weaving together of the different instruments' sounds and tones, the vibrations that penetrate the body... Soon enough you are filled with the music and you don't know where you begin or end—you become the music.

When you were just born, you experienced the world and yourself as one symphony. Notice, without naming and labeling the experience, it is just the same now. You are aware of the symphony of this experience:

sensing,

feeling,

hearing,

seeing...

just like a newborn baby,

no "I" thought.

Nothing has changed in being an *adult*. Only thinking has been added to the experience. Life performs just a more complex symphony:

sensing,

feeling,

hearing,

seeing,

thinking...

There is awareness of this symphony. Turn your mind to the awareness itself. What are you?

8.7 NOTICE THE UNCHANGING QUALITY PRESENT IN ANY EXPERIENCE

Relax and sit quietly, not straining at all, not in the physical body, not in the mind, not in the eyes. Relax. Sit simply with no agenda and imagine looking from the eyes that are on the back of your head. This view includes the surroundings, and also your own body.

Notice that if you experience any type of discomfort or bodily tension, there is a knowingness of the bodily tension. And a knowingness of energy, if you're sensitive to energy movements. And a knowingness of the body and the environment.

Simple knowingness, presence.

This presence is very unassuming and intimate with everything. Notice how, even though everything is even slightly changing and in movement, this knowingness itself does not fluctuate at all. It is so essential, it is just there, a silent witness.

Remember the mirror I polished in my room at the retreat and in which I saw perfectly clear images? This knowingness reminds me of such a mirror, a silent witness of reflections. The world displays itself in a clear space of consciousness like reflections in a mirror.

This is not the thinking mind *observer:* a state of being deliberately mindful to everything in the experience. In fact, if you notice an observer, drop it. Turn your attention to the noticing itself, merging intimately with the experience. I know it is not easy. The years of habitual practice of observing and practicing mindfulness are not easy to let go of. But try this: just sit and breathe. Sit and breathe. Do not *observe* sitting and breathing. Imagine yourself as a boy or a girl and just sit as a boy or a girl, not like a spiritual seeker who has developed the habit of observing from a distance. Sit like a boy. Or a girl. Just sit. If you notice you are striving to see, to understand, to experience, just relax. Relax even the slightest striving. Be still. Do nothing. The knowingness reveals itself; there is no need to try to find it. Just notice that you know you are sitting. You know you are breathing. There is the presence of this knowingness that is always there. Notice that this knowingness holds all appearances, just as a mirror also holds them. Unchanged by appearances, by the world of objects, a presence-mirror, a silent space for all existence, is always here.

AFTERWORD TO PART 2

When you arrive, you KNOW. No one needs
to tell you that you are home. You recognize it, you
feel it, you just know it. You take off your hat, your
boots... You sit. The fire warms your face; your hands
rest on your lap. You know there is really nothing to
search for anymore. You are home. You feel the joy
of being, you dance and run around... You trip and
fall—and curse the heavens...You laugh, you cry, you
sit and watch the fire... You know you can just *be*...
You know you are home.

You have been here all along, but something
always called you to search for it. All this time, you
were sitting in front of your fireplace, but so engaged
in the stories of the mind that you felt as if you were

somewhere else and needed to find your way back home. Sudden recognition of this simple truth stops the search immediately.

MY LOVE AND GRATITUDE TO

All the Teachers that supported me in various ways on my journey, directly and indirectly, thank you for crossing my path either with your presence or with your words.

Anthony Mondragon - my Beloved Native American partner whom I met in Big Sur, California. You grounded my energies when I settled with you after several years of nomadic life. You gave me the space to unwind old mind patterns after awakening, and to be completely authentic within our relationship; I could then step into the world in a brave way with my work. My next book will include the story of your unusual path to awakening, our auspicious meeting, and the impact of it on our lives and the lives of others.

Daniel Aliyev - my precious son. You chose to be born out of me, to be deeply conditioned by me as a part of your journey in this lifetime. I can't undo anything, but I can be honest in my own life journey and with myself, and maybe this will help you to shed the mounds of beliefs that were imprinted on you by my own ignorance. You always will be my Zaya. I love you so much!

Pasha - my ex-husband, my Dharma partner in seeking enlightenment. We were so lost and so deeply conditioned that we matched like two peas in a pod to bring both of us to such an unbearable suffering that liberation became possible! I will always be grateful for everything we lived together—through thick and thin—and I miss you!

Jane Murphy - my dedicated editor and curious friend. You recognized my storytelling gift in one of the writing gatherings where I read an excerpt from this book, and came to me after to express your surprise and wonder. We became playful partners to bring this book out of the dungeons of my computer's hard drive to a reality. I am forever grateful for your help, Seal!

Mark Marshall and **Frederic Constant** - my support team. You incorporated my early work of awakening inquiry, *Direct Pointing*, expanded it and established Nonduality Forum, where you offer guidance to release the illusion of separation and encourage to live an authentic life. It helps me to focus solely on post-awakening support, knowing that there are resources available to help people to wake up! You also, along with Jane Murphy, helped me to edit this book. The book would not have happened without your dedication; thank you!

Bonnie Aungle - my friend and "a fairy" (at least this is how I always remember you from our meeting in your forest dwelling in Australia). We met in the on-line forum Ruthless Truth in 2010 and worked, along with others, on the creation of Liberation Unleashed. I am grateful to you for designing with me the Buddha on a Bull image and this book cover - and the next one too!

Tina Paytek - my friend who lives on "a Garden of Eden" ranch in Texas and who is here to teach people how to unburden and simplify their lives! I appreciate your dedication to my website, even when I had zero visitors. You kept updating it, migrating it, and did whatever was needed to keep it going, so now people can find me easily and read about my work.

Fergus Denhamer — my deep heart friend. I met you through Liberation Unleashed in the early 2012 and you actually made a trip to meet me in person in 2018 in Big Sur, California! We spent time together floating in the mineral waters of the magical Esalen, walking in the gardens, and sharing our journeys. This meeting enabled me to step forward into opening up my expression fully and courageously, which made possible the many things that followed in my life.

Lori Lothian - the awake lunatic of "Lunatic Astrology," discussions with you about your astrology and my Human Design studies grew my intention to publish a series of books on awakening. As we both know, this "Mental Projector" is here in this lifetime to do just that! And thank you for the brilliant back cover copy!

Chris Grosso - one cool dude at Be Here Now Network. Thank you for your passionate foreword which you agreed to write at the last minute, inspired by reading the book! And you immediately inspired others to read it.

A friend of mine: "Wow...that review makes me want to go out and buy ten copies!"

Me: "That's what 'good shit' does!"

Nurit and **Gabor Harsanyi** - spiritual friends. Thank you for your heartfelt foreword! Meeting you in your office - a coffee shop in the center of Budapest - was the most delightful meeting! Dear Gabor, I suddenly met a heart friend, awake and at the same time settled in his own humanity, who is unafraid to look silly and ordinary. I loved the childlike nature we very much share! I will wholeheartedly recommend you as a spiritual mentor. Dear Nurit, you became a role model for me to publish books myself and to embrace the freedom of independent publishing! Thank you so much for your generous support!

Vinito Freo - my heart friend across the Pacific ocean! Thank you for riding with me on a Bull as my first reader and helping me when I was making final fine-tuning to a manuscript. Loving you!

Jane Green - the book designer I feel so lucky to have found! It has been an absolute pleasure to work with you on *Buddha on a Bull*! Professional, quick, creative, solution oriented, you met all my various demands and answered my endless questions with ease, calm and positivity! Thank you for being patient with my every "final" subtitle until the very end!

My love and gratitude to everyone who read this book before the release and shared with me your feedback, sentiments, endorsements and testimonials!

To connect with Elena please follow her Facebook Author's page *Complete Humanity Project*.

Also, you may be interested to join the community of people who value authentic expression and courageous living. Look for *Complete Humanity Community* group on Facebook!

You can also visit *www.ElenaNezhinsky.com* and her blog *Complete Humanity* to learn of her latest adventures.

ABOUT THE AUTHOR

Elena is an independent thinker and a long-time seeker of Truth.

She was one of the co-founders of a global awakening movement called Liberation Unleashed and she is a co-creator of the spiritual inquiry method of *Direct Pointing* that can lead to release the illusion of separation.

From guiding people to awakening, over time Elena's focus has shifted towards helping with integration of the awakening experience. From her own experience with post-awakening Elena developed a method of grounding the energies after awakening and embracing the two levels of existence—absolute and human—for a fulfilling, meaningful life. You may learn about this work at www.ElenaNezhinsky.com

Elena's diverse background includes a Master's degree in Engineering, certifications in professional coaching and many holistic health modalities. She has studied Behavioral Psychology extensively. She is an empath and has auditory psychic abilities that are an essential part of her mentorship and coaching work.

Born in the small ancient town-fort of Ostrog in Eastern Ukraine, Elena came to the United States in 1992 and lived in New York City for nearly 25 years. She loves the Monterey, California area and, with her partner Anthony, has made her home there since 2015. She has a grown-up son, Daniel.

Since childhood, Elena has been deeply connected to

Nature. She admires the beauty of the Pacific Coast and loves walks on the beach and in the forest. She is an avid listener of classical music, enjoys riding her bicycle around town and loves spending time alone in contemplation.

CPSIA information can be obtained
at www.ICGtesting.com
Printed in the USA
FSHW010703061019
62742FS